"One of the greatest contemporary Catholic philosophers, an intellectual concerned with politics and attentive to the unique reality of persons and things, humble before what is objective and thus opened to the truth. One great theme dominates De Corte's work the subjects of which are only apparently divergent: the vigorous denunciation of modern rationalism and an invitation to man to renew a bond with reality, without which he cannot live as a man. De Corte is above all a moralist and a philosopher of the state of crisis. As he himself declared, two subjects haunted him as a philosopher, the crisis of society and the crisis of the Church."

— **DANILO CASTELLANO**, Italian philosopher and author whose works include *L'aristotelismo cristiano di Marcel de Corte*

"One of the greatest twentieth-century masters of the counterrevolution." De Corte waged a battle of the intellect "against the current 'dis-society' of modern democracy, totalitarianism of the state, and the consumer society, and, at the same time, for the restoration of man in the fullness of his relationship to God, the world around us, and our neighbors. A brave, tireless warrior."

— **JUAN VALLET DE GOYTISOLO**, Spanish jurist and philosopher, author, among other works, of *Ideología, praxis y mito de la tecnocracia.*

"For centuries, since the moral insights of Plato and Aristotle, the virtues were considered as the heart of morality. To be good meant cultivating virtue, a training of intellect and will toward goodness which affected even the body. Morality was not conceived merely as a dry adherence to external rules but as a change of life, a true internal transformation. It is this which Marcel De Corte, with so many lively and interesting comments on contemporary society, brings to life in this series of books. They are an important contribution to what is known today as 'virtue ethics,' a cultivation of the soul as old nearly as philosophy but just as important for our moral life today."

—**THOMAS STORCK**, author, editor and translator, most recently author of *Economics: An Alternative Introduction* (XIII Books)

"The image of De Corte, obtained from his writings in *Itinéraires*, has remained with me, with his devastating analysis of: the epistemological reversal of modernity; the derangement of what is the product of this, the 'homo rationalis'; the irredeemable crisis of civilization; the corrupting character of politics founded on the 'religion of democracy,' and the tragedy which was—and still is—the crisis of the post-conciliar Church. De Corte, of an unsurpassed intellectual mettle, professed philosophical realism which is in perfect accord with his anti-modernism. The denial of an uncreated order of values leads to modernism and ends by negating tradition, religion and morality."

—**MIGUEL AYUSO**, Professor of Political Science at the Comillas Pontifical University, Madrid, and author of books on social and political topics, most recently, of *¿El pueblo contra el Estado?*

FORTITUDE

ortitude

MARCEL DE CORTE
Translated by Inez Fitzgerald Storck

AROUCA
PRESS

Taken from the 3rd edition published in 2019 by
Dominique Martin Morin (Poitiers, France).
This English edition also includes copious
footnotes by the translator.

ISBN: 978-1-998492-56-5

Arouca Press
PO Box 55003
Bridgeport PO
Waterloo, ON N2J 3G0
Canada
www.aroucapress.com
Send inquiries to info@aroucapress.com

Cover illustration from a print
of the Four Virtues by
Hendrick Goltzius (1558–1617)

CONTENTS

TRANSLATOR'S INTRODUCTION

Marcel De Corte and the Vatican II Revolution

I N THIS VOLUME, AS IN OTHER works, Marcel De Corte issues a strong indictment against the post-Conciliar Catholic Church: "It is undeniable that a 'new Christianity' has insinuated itself within the bosom of the Church..." This secularized Christianity, centered on man, has adopted the attitudes of the modern world. A pivotal document of Vatican II, *Gaudium et Spes* (*GS*) "echoes the belief, today spread over the whole earth, that man is the culmination of the universe, and calls for the religion of man to be integrated into Catholicism." De Corte even refers to this document in a footnote as "the compilation of all the modern forms of insanity."

How are we to assess this bold condemnation? First, we must note that to devout Catholics of De Corte's generation, the changes in the Church appeared to be a rupture. A wave of enthusiasm for change swept over many of the bishops, clergy, and laity. While the documents of Vatican II can all be read within a hermeneutic of continuity, there are emphases that advocate a new approach to confronting and engaging with contemporary society. To read in *GS* an injunction to enter into dialogue with mankind about such problems as "the meaning of individual and collective endeavor" and "the destiny of nature and of men" (no. 3) must have seemed lacking in relevance to those who held that the answer to current problems was simply to proclaim the Gospel with greater vigor and zeal. Granted, the Council aimed to address society's needs in the light of the Gospel, but with a focus on solidarity and cooperation. This stance seemingly vitiated the traditional belief that the Church transmits to people what is necessary for their salvation and a correct understanding of suffering and death. To someone like De Corte, who believed in the hierarchical structure of the Church (as well as society), the new approach seemed off the mark.

While *GS* makes clear that there can be no understanding of human anthropology without an understanding of the Word made flesh (no. 22), it would have sounded odd to De Corte to hear an appeal for "fraternal dialogue" and a "deeper level of personal fellowship" (no. 23) with no reference to shared Christian beliefs as a basis for such interchanges. Similarly, the document asserts that when "individuals and groups practice moral and social virtues and foster them in social living," then with the help of grace "there will arise a generation of new men, the molders of a new humanity" (no. 30). But if this "new humanity" is not founded on the Church, it will be a house built on

sand and there will be no true renewal of man. It is
not "an unquenchable thirst for human dignity" that
the "ferment of the Gospel has aroused" (no. 26), but
a thirst for the living God. Otherwise the Gospel is
distorted and perverted, turned upside down, putting
the glory of man before the glory of God.

De Corte would have approved of the call to respect
the common good, but not subordinating it to the
good of the person (no. 26). This, De Corte maintains,
would be putting the cart before the horse. As he
tirelessly repeats, when the ultimate end of personal
and societal activities is the common good, the individual benefits from living in a healthy community.

Perhaps it is easier to understand De Corte's vis-
ceral reaction to *GS* since we have now seen that
an approach of dialogue and partnership has not
advanced the spread of the Gospel. Au contraire.
Actually, in some areas where Catholics are persecuted,
where no dialogue is possible, such as large sections
of Nigeria, the Church is flourishing and seminaries
are full, even as future priests fully understand that
they may be persecuted and martyred.

In addition, De Corte witnessed: misguided
attempts on the part of bishops and priests to engage
with the modern world, such as clerics enamored of
socialism and communism; acceptance of the world-
view of Teilhard de Chardin; and the blurring of the
distinction between nature and grace by influential
theologians. Paul VI did not always defend doctrinal
clarity, as when he backed down when the Dutch
bishops refused to accept the Holy See's corrections

to *A New Catechism*, an early and influential compen-
dium which contained doctrinal errors. The French
bishops' *Pierres Vivantes* (*Living Stones*), a collection of catechetical texts for children issued in 1981,
also contained doctrinal errors, such as presenting
the Resurrection less as a historical fact than the
product of the experience of the apostles. Vatican
censors demanded corrections, which, when made,
did not entirely meet with their approval. De Corte
also disapproved of misplaced ecumenical activities,
and would undoubtedly have opposed the interfaith
prayer meeting convened by John Paul II in Assisi in
1986, which gave the appearance of supporting false
religions. As De Corte observed all this, he could
only characterize the council with its aftermath as
a colossal failure, with its use of indecisive language,
removed from traditional theological terminology and
open to various interpretations, and its hesitancy in
proclaiming the identity of the Church founded by
Christ with the Catholic Church (see *Lumen Gentium*
no. 8, which states that the Church of Christ "subsists
in the Catholic Church.").

Nor was De Corte less harsh in his condemnation
of the Novus Ordo, subject to "all the whims of the
ringmaster and entertainment producer," as he charac-
terizes it in *Fortitude*. Yet he faithfully attended a liturgy he regarded as Protestantized, sometimes sitting
behind a pillar to distance himself from it. He refused
to support Archbishop Marcel Lefebvre, even though
he and the priests of his community, the Society of St.
Pius X, continued to celebrate the traditional Latin

Mass. De Corte voiced his criticisms of the new Mass in the French journal *Itinéraires*, founded and edited by Jean Madiran, who also deplored it. In a letter to Madiran published in *Itinéraires* in February 1970, De Corte admitted that he was tempted more than once to leave the Church because the "demolition project" of the Novus Ordo retained so little of the traditional liturgy and downplayed the concept of the Mass as a sacrifice. Other major contributors to the journal expressed similar assessments.

Throughout his commentary on the decline in society, which runs throughout his volumes on the cardinal virtues, De Corte links the advent of a dis-society to the secularization of the Church. When the supernatural is not held in esteem, the natural becomes debased. The religion of humanity, incarnate in De Corte's eyes in liberal democracy and communism, imitates Christianity with its "counterfeit of supernatural grace" (*Prudence*), human ties which supplant the mystical bonds uniting the members of the Body of Christ.

This desperate situation can only be reversed slowly, by building up society and the common good through the virtue of fortitude and the other cardinal virtues. The loss of these virtues has entailed the evisceration of their true meaning. Prudence comes to signify astuteness in dealing with others, a self-protecting caution. With regard to justice, "Never has general justice, wrongly called 'social justice,' been so thoroughly emptied of its meaning. What is called 'social justice' today is nothing other than its reverse. It is the process whereby an individual, isolated or aggregated with others, demands his due of others, instead of rendering to them what is due them." And there is no particular justice (distributive or commutative) without general justice (see *Justice* for an elaboration of these concepts). On the distortion of fortitude, De Corte writes in this volume: "Fortitude no longer exists as a virtue ordered towards the common good. Reduced to a mere principle of action, it no longer plays a role in human conduct except under the guise of violence or apathy..." At its extreme, fortitude degenerates into "its caricature: revolutionary violence." With regard to temperance, this virtue has disappeared in a world given over to the delights offered to the consumer, where modern "society" is evolving towards what would be called "the dis-society of pleasure" (*Temperance*, to appear).

De Corte makes an ardent appeal for the return to the practice of the cardinal virtues, which should be preached by the clergy and included in catechetical materials. They enable us to assess the means and the ends required to attain our own personal good in this world and the next and the common good of society. If these virtues continue to be downplayed in the Church and relegated to oblivion in society, there will be no hope of replacing the current dis-society with a just social order. Our civilization will disappear, with no legacy to hand on to whatever form of political and social life will come next. This is a terrifying prospect.

Inez Fitzgerald Storck

I

FORTITUDE IN A WORLD WITHOUT JUSTICE OR PRUDENCE

AMONG THE CARDINAL VIR-
tues, on which hinge all properly human
activities directed towards the good,
fortitude fares no better today than
prudence and justice—nor, as we
shall later see, than temperance.[1]
Its fate is, in fact, even worse. Prudence, reduced
to the paltry role of cautious attentiveness in driving
or crossing the street, still retains, however minutely,
something of its original status and its functions of
counsel, judgment, and governance. Justice, until not
long ago still oriented towards the common good of
men in society, is now increasingly focused on the good
of the individual and of individuals grouped together
in coalitions of every kind, bloated to the bursting
point like the fabulist's frog.[2] In contradistinction,

---

[1] On the current debasement of justice and prudence, see our
studies *De la Prudence* and *De la Justice* (*Prudence* and *Justice*,
published by Arouca Press in 2024 and 2025 respectively).
[2] A reference to a fable, going back to Aesop, in which a frog
bursts as it tries to inflate itself to the size of an ox. Jean de La

fortitude no longer exists as a virtue ordered towards the good. Reduced to a mere principle of physical or mental action, it no longer plays a role in human conduct except under the guise of violence or apathy, both of which debase it to the level of beasts.

Deprived of the necessary support of prudence and justice, fortitude is no longer a moral virtue or a cardinal virtue. It is no longer a virtue that *transcends* the individual and directs him towards the common good of the polity and the common good of the world, which is God. However, when an individual pursues this ultimate earthly good, he himself then becomes perfected: as a natural consequence, he is able to participate in all the other goods encompassed within this overarching earthly good, which society transmits through space and time; as a supernatural consequence, he is granted, according to his zeal in loving God above all things, the possession of divine life within the Mystical Body of Christ, which is the Church.

Fortitude is no longer one of the drivers of the *quadriga*[3] of the cardinal virtues. Instead, as bitter experience attests, fortitude has become a principle of bestial brutality or reactive intimidation, which stifles what remains of social life in a fragmented world, as well as within the Church, now beset by the "communitarian" delirium.

At the root of this degradation of the virtue of fortitude into the "will to power"—whose still-embryonic

Fontaine (1621–1695), a French poet primarily known for his fables, included this tale in his collection.

[3] In Greek and Roman times, a chariot led by four horses.

presence in the world of his time Nietzsche celebrated, without foreseeing that it would secrete around itself, to secure its triumph, an enormous bureaucratic carapace that would render powerless all those subjected to its impersonal pressures — lies the slow and now accelerated mutation of human societies into *dis-societies* through the pressure of individualism. This individualism stems from a *desupernaturalized*, secularized Christianity, amputated from its essential relation to God, Creator of the universe and Savior of men.

The historical stages of this process are well known: the humanism of the Renaissance, the rejection by the Reformation of the existence of a Church as the custodian of revelation, and the collapse of the society of the Ancien Régime due to the fierce attacks of political, economic, and social liberalism — whose ultimate outcome can only be what Paul Valéry foresaw as the "perfect and definitive ant colony,"[4] towards which we are blindly advancing.

We cannot emphasize too much that for nearly four centuries, we have gradually lost the concept of the *common good*, the cornerstone of general justice, which orders the members of a society to their collective whole, just as parts are ordered to a whole, or as many different musicians follow the conductor in an orchestra. From general justice,[5] distributive justice immediately follows, assigning each citizen his place within the community according to the services he

---

[4] Paul Valéry (1871–1945), French poet and philosopher. The citation is from *Variété I*, 1924.
[5] I.e., legal justice.

renders, ensuring that unity, mutual understanding, harmony, and friendship prevail.

In this whole, all parts are indeed parts; they are all, in this sense, equal, and they fulfill the fundamental requirement of justice, which requires equality. However, this equality is geometric, as it was once called — it is proportional to the diversity and hierarchy of functions that are actually assumed and that complement each other. In modern times, however, all that remains is commutative justice, governed by arithmetic equality and by the law of fair exchange (*quid pro quo*), which dominates economic transactions, which according to their fundamental objective all ultimately lead to the consumer, an individual of flesh and blood, the only being truly capable of acquiring material goods in exchange for payment.

The time is coming, if it has not already arrived, when the planet will become the base of a vast corporation for the distribution of material goods produced by humanity for its sustenance, which, since it is *linked to the body*, is necessarily *individualized*. This "society" will bring together human beings who conform to the definition of the individual as *separated from his fellow men: ab omni divisum.*[6] This will be the death of true society.

How is such a future, such a present, possible? To this question, there is only one answer: a civilization such as ours, which has spread across the entire globe, uniting all nations with their various forms of politics,

---

[6] Separated from all.

economics, and social life, quite similar despite their differences, antagonisms, conflicts, and even their cold wars, cannot easily rid itself of the Christianity that presided over its birth. This remains true despite the separation of Church and state, despite the professed atheism or religious indifference of the civilization.

Onto a society composed of an immense variety of micro-societies, and, in the last analysis, of *naturally social beings* from their birth to their death — for example, a family or a people, is not made up of individuals, except quantitatively, but of a father, a mother, of Frenchmen, Belgians, etc. — Christianity has superimposed (in the strict sense of the word, from above) a unique and unprecedented form of society, *composed of persons*. In light of their ultimate supernatural end, social distinctions are truly set aside, for, as St. Paul says, "There is no longer Jew or Greek" (Gal. 3:28; Col. 3:11). We enter the Church *one by one*, personally, through baptism, independently of any membership in a particular collectivity. And if we are saved — always personally — it is in Christ Himself, who will be "all in all" (Col. 3:11), uniting all persons to each other within His Mystical Body in its perfected state, which is the Church Triumphant. In anticipation of this, and in a way that is at once more hidden and yet visible, this same reality is realized in the Church Militant here below, through grace, the *Credo*, the sacraments, and the Holy Sacrifice of the Mass.

The two societies, natural and ecclesial, are each perfect in the way that they are ordered, but the essential difference in their structures does not prevent them from offering mutual support. Natural society disseminates, through its thousands of channels, the evangelical message of which the Church is the guardian, while the grace diffused by the ecclesial institution reinforces the social nature of man. The numerous tensions between the Church and the state, reaching their climax in the Middle Ages during the struggles between the papacy and the empire, do not alter this fact: these were border conflicts, violent yet incidental, rather than reciprocal denials of their respective natures.

There is no other cause of the emergence of secularized societies in the modern era — societies that are, in fact, dis-societies — than the loss of the sense of the supernatural within the soul of man. This is accompanied by the substitution of anthropocentrism for theocentrism, which had been professed in Christian and even pagan ages. The inevitable consequence of this shift is the desupernaturalization of the human person, who is raised up to be both principle and end of all human acts, and the glorification of the good pertaining to the individual, to which the entire social order must now be subjected. This individual good is nothing more than an artificial construct, a work of man — the individual man, for there is no other — which will function like a machine for his benefit.

Who does not recognize in the primacy given today to a society based on economics — one that revolves around individuals or groups of individuals and assimilates into itself all that is social and political and necessary for a truly human life — a mere projection onto the purely earthly plane of the ecclesial society of persons, but now secularized and composed of elements that aspire only to their own personal good?

In such a milieu, there is no longer the slightest place for general justice and the primacy of the common good, nor for distributive justice, *nor for the virtue of fortitude, which would otherwise uphold the social order for which it serves as a foundational support.* The devaluation of the virtue of justice inevitably brings about the devaluation of the virtue of fortitude, and this, in turn, is itself caused by the decline of supernatural faith in God, Creator of the universe and Savior of humanity, the Common Good of all that exists, of all who think and have desires.

There is then nothing left—let us repeat this tirelessly, for it is the key to modern history—but the human person, who, left to himself and seeking his own individual good, thereby breaks his allegiance to the primacy of the common good of the natural and semi-natural societies to which he belongs by birth or vocation. In doing so, he will inevitably attempt, without ever succeeding, to artificially construct a "new society" *based on the only model he possesses*, yet one whose supernatural transcendence he rejects: the ecclesial institution. Lacking the virtue of fortitude, he is incapable of achieving this task. All that remains is its caricature: revolutionary violence.

This is why we have entered into an age of permanent revolution, one that seeks to establish an impossible communism—which, if one is willing to open one's eyes, exists nowhere except in name—where the state takes the place of God. Pascal stated it clearly: "Force without justice is tyrannical."[7] The misfortune, however, is that this tyranny is now faceless, painless, omnipresent, and provokes only those revolts or upheavals that expand its domain. Its universal coercion even causes it to be loved by all.

Prudence, which concerns deliberation about, selection of, and direction of the effective means for the realization of the common good, the source of all other goods, disappears along with the neglect of general justice. No longer directed towards the common good, prudence ceases to be grounded in reality, resulting in a profound distortion parallel to the one we have already noted in the relationship between justice and fortitude, a distortion that now affects fortitude itself.

Fortitude, which is indispensable to prudence in order to achieve the common good of unity—always precarious in this fallen world since the Fall—no longer has any reason to be objective, which would validate it and provide it with its ultimate goal. It withdraws into the *self*, without any end that transcends and guides it. It has no other goal than the unlimited evolution of the human person—hence, the myth of progress—or the unlimited growth of a class, of groups of individuals, who are ceaselessly at work, violently annihilating everything that opposes them.

To love the common good, from which prudence derives its impetus and orientation—allowing it to

---

[7] *Pensées*, 1670.

adhere *with fortitude* to the means that ensure the realization of the common good — becomes incomprehensible and pointless. The highest form of prudence, "the most perfect of all," as St. Thomas writes, is *political prudence ordered to the common good of unity by the virtue of justice.* To political prudence, he states, *"it belongs to govern and command,"*[8] and to have recourse to fortitude, since this mission is beset with all kinds of obstacles, to the point of requiring, if necessary, as we shall see, the citizen to sacrifice his life for it. Fortitude will be replaced by bureaucratic red tape, reinforced by police coercion.

Now there is no more need for fortitude, guided by reason, to maintain men ordered to and observant of the common good, while mobilizing their capacity to resist the evils that assail all temporal societies. Instead, it is enough to promise them the *satisfaction of their material needs,* which are inseparable from their *individual selves,* each engaged in pursuing his own individual good. "Liberal" ideology does this by constructing the "consumer society" and the "permissive society," while *communist ideology* does so by building the "totalitarian society" and the prospect of a new earthly paradise where the desires of one and all will be completely fulfilled.

In both cases, we witness the vertical collapse of the virtues of justice and prudence, and also of fortitude, without which the final ends of these virtues can never be realized. Because the common good no longer

---

[8] *Summa Theologiae* (hereafter *ST*), II-II, q. 50, art. 1, c.; *Commentary on Aristotle's Nicomachean Ethics* (hereafter *CNE*), 1196.

exists, society itself ceases to exist. What remains is a dis-society — either teeming with chaos or stagnant, depending on the circumstances — veneered with the illusion of *a dream* or *utopia*.

Let us not be deceived: the "consumer society" and the communist earthly paradise are far less materialistic than one might suppose. The greed of the consumer self or the self that aspires to be the sole god of the new Eden is a *mental construct*, one which perpetually looks to a future that exists only in the mind. It is never satisfied, never fulfilled, never real. It perishes at every moment, only to be reborn a moment later, and so on ad infinitum. It is *imaginary*, pure becoming, without ever existing. This illusion only sustains itself through relentless advertising, enticing displays of consumer goods, bombardments of propaganda; their *ubiquity mimics the omnipresence of reality*, takes its place, vacating it and presenting itself to the mind as the only thing that really exists. At times

> *The imagination that preparing for its orgy*
> *Finds nothing but a reef at the break of*
> *dawn*[9]

but more often, the mystified mind surrenders to its own falsehoods, feeds on its own delusions, and encloses the self, or the many faces of the self, within itself, drawing everything from itself and referring everything back to itself.

How, in such an atmosphere, could there still be openness to the realism inherent in the virtue

---

[9] "Le Voyage" in Baudelaire's *Les Fleurs du mal* (1857).

of fortitude, which, as Aquinas states, "endures and repels grave dangers, in which it is most difficult to remain steadfast"?[10] Fortitude involves resistance, either to a hostile external world or to an adversarial *other* that threatens the *authentic nature* of the human being—that is, that which essentially defines him within the order of action: his status as a "political animal," a member of a polity or of a whole that gives him his very life. Once cut off from the common good—the principle that orients all other real goods, whether natural or supernatural—the human person, now fallen into his own inner emptiness, has no recourse but to abandon himself to his dreams.

No one, in such a case, resists the seductions of the madwoman in the attic, the imagination, now further stirred up by envy, itself a phenomenon of the mind that intensifies these deceptions. The *self*, exasperated when confronted with a social world that no longer conveys an engaging, efficacious dynamism, can do nothing but substitute for the virtue of fortitude the vehemence of pure passions, always internal, such as rage, jealousy, covetousness, and hatred. These passions mask themselves beneath the cloak of social ideologies, which fabricate illusions from the "Isles of the Blessed"[11] to conceal their harmful effects.

The manipulation of the weak by fanatics, the hard-hearted, the deceitful, and the Machiavellian becomes nothing more than a mass-produced technique. As

---

[10] *ST*, II-II, q. 123, art. 2, c.
[11] Or "Fortunate Isles," legendary paradisiacal islands in Greek mythology.

Simone Weil observes, modern slavery has even suc-
ceeded in making itself loved by those who endure
it.[12] How could it be otherwise for all those who no
longer draw their fortitude from the virtues of justice
and prudence, virtues directly related to the surest and
most human of ends that man, as a political animal,
can realize here below: the common good?[13] The self
may seek refuge in a group to recover the appearance of
power, but nothing is more malleable than the masses.

If it is true that the bankruptcy—or more precisely, the fraudulent bankruptcy—of general justice
and prudence in the modern era, and their replace-
ment by all too familiar counterfeits, have led to
the disappearance of the virtue of fortitude, which
had been sustained by these virtues, the converse
is even more true: in the concrete order of things,
without fortitude neither prudence nor justice can
exist. There is no prudence, no rectitude of practical reason with regard to its end, its deliberations,
its choices, or its injunctions, without the virtue of
fortitude, which enables it to take action, aligns it
with reality, and wards off the constant deformation
it faces in this fallen world due to the influence of
short-term interests, temporal advantages, and all that
human subjectivity craves. There is no general justice,
the queen of all the virtues, without the virtue of

---

[12] See *Réflexions sur les causes de la liberté et de l'oppression* (1934)
in *Oppression et liberté* (1955).
[13] Aristotle, *Nicomachean Ethics* (henceforth *Nic. Eth.*), I, 1,
1094b: *Finis politicae est humanum bonum, id est optimus in
rebus humanis* (The end of political science is the good of man,
what is best in human affairs).

fortitude, without the judicious authority of law and its guardians, who, through sound discipline, orient all human acts toward their ultimate end here below: the common good of unity, the pathway to all other goods. "Fortitude has a general utility, which is to preserve the entire order of justice," as St. Thomas teaches, with his sound judgment.[14]

Indeed, it belongs to *virtue* to ensure that man is good and that his actions conform to his nature as a political animal, that is, to reason, which only develops within a social life. But to achieve this, three conditions are necessary:

1. Reason itself must be rightly ordered — this is the role of the intellectual virtues, of which prudence is foremost in the domain of action.

2. Right reason must permeate human relationships; this is the role of justice.

3. The obstacles to the influence of prudence and justice must be eliminated.

There are two obstacles that prevent the will from following the dictates of right reason:

1. The first is the lure of a pleasurable good that incites one to act contrary to right reason; this must be overcome by temperance.[15]

2. The second is the aversion of the will toward that which is reasonable yet difficult; here, fortitude must intervene, holding out against the setbacks that incline the soul toward inertia, just as physical strength overcomes and removes material obstacles.

[14] *ST*, II-II, q. 123, art. 12, ad 5.
[15] See De Corte's *Temperance*, to be published by Arouca Press.

It follows, then, that fortitude is not only a virtue required for man to act in accordance with reason, but also that it holds the third place in the hierarchy of virtues, immediately after prudence, the perfection of reason, and justice (both general and particular), which implements the dictates of reason in society according to the order established by reason. Maintaining the proper arrangement of the parts within the whole — parts which are always tempted to break away due to the passions that assail human weakness — belongs *above all* to fortitude. To carry out what should be done, courage is always *of the first necessity*.

If the order of precedence among the cardinal virtues is indeed: prudence, justice, fortitude, and temperance, followed by the cortege of other virtues,[16] then in *putting them into practice* — without which there is neither virtue nor common or individual good — fortitude is the condition of all virtue and all good. "For it is essential for a virtue to act with firmness and consistency," especially when, with regard to fortitude, it is a matter of "enduring and repelling grave dangers, in which it is most difficult to remain steadfast," as we have seen above. This is where we find the specific object of fortitude.[17]

Every virtue has recourse to fortitude. Fortitude is truly itself in the presence of danger and temporal evils that divert man from the exercise of the cardinal virtues, of which prudence and justice are the focal points.

[16] *ST*, II-II, q. 123, art. 12, c.
[17] *ST*, II-II, q. 123, art. 2, c.

II

THE NATURE OF THE VIRTUE OF FORTITUDE

A VIRTUE LIKE ANY OTHER, that is to say, with the character, modus operandi, and principle of action common to all virtues, fortitude is also a unique virtue due to its own end: removing obstacles that prevent the will from obeying practical reason as it is guided by prudence and justice. In the face of an evil that is *difficult to overcome*, every man naturally experiences fear. He recoils from certain sufferings, severe trials, great misfortunes, serious illnesses, and death, which afflict him because he belongs to the animal kingdom, for whom such is the inescapable lot. The pure Act that is God does not suffer at all; He experiences no passion or receptivity to external impressions. Outside of God, every being is, in fact, capable of suffering, even the angels. In this regard, man has the highest degree of receptivity, since his soul receives everything from the outside through the mediation of the body.

When man is confronted with something that troubles, threatens, or endangers him, his sensory perception passes into his soul, and he then strives either to withstand it or to fight against it *with all his might*, as the common expression so aptly puts it. A formidable evil is one that ought to be avoided, for it acts as a repelling force, to which it is the function of fear to respond. Yet it also warrants being confronted, for it offers man the opportunity to overcome it and thereby to be freed from it; this is the function of audacity. These two passions, classified as *irascible* by the ancients, are instinctively felt by animals.[1] They are natural dispositions located in the sensitive appetite. In man, the movements of these passions, which correspond to the biological necessity of preserving himself in existence, are not in themselves good or evil; they become good when regulated by reason, and evil when they escape its governance. To fear without reason or to rush into danger without measuring the risks is not the mark of a man worthy of the name, endowed with intelligence and will.

As St. Thomas writes with admirable clarity, "The virtue of fortitude has as its function the removal of obstacles that prevent the will from obeying reason.

---

[1] There is also, as we shall see in *Temperance*, a form of passion proceeding from the sensitive appetite that consists of desiring an object pleasing to the body or experiencing a repugnance towards it if it is not good for the body. This type of passion is termed *concupiscible*. It concerns the pleasurable and the painful. On the irascible appetite, see *ST*, I-II, q. 23, art 2; and, also by Aquinas, *De Veritate*, q. 26, art. 4. Of the greatest interest is a work by C. Cvinklinski and A. Serralda, *Pavlov, pour un renouveau de la culture*, Paris, 1979, which shows to what degree the biological function of *defense* (having to the with the irascible appetite) is critical and fundamental in human life, and (we add) to what point the philosophical theory of form touching the deepest roots of the material in the living is conformed to the latest discoveries in experimental biology.

Now to shrink before a difficulty is proper to fear, which causes one to retreat in the face of an evil *that is difficult to overcome....* Fortitude, therefore, mainly has to do with the *fear* of difficulties, which has the potential to prevent the will from being faithful to reason. Moreover, it is necessary not only to stand firm against the assault of these difficulties by restraining fear, but also to confront them with moderation (*moderate*) when it becomes necessary to overcome them in order to secure the future. This seems to pertain to the nature of audacity. Fortitude, therefore, concerns both fear and audacity, to moderate the former and to restrain the latter."[2]

---

[2] *ST*, II-II, q. 123, art. 3, c.; *Nich. Eth.* III, 1, 1110a. The meaning that Aristotle and St. Thomas give to moderation, involving a sense of proportion, must not be misunderstood. *Moderate* in no way means *not very intense, quite weak*, as one would be inclined to believe today. *Measured* does not mean *constrained* or *slow*. Neither does moderation imply the total elimination of fear: "You tremble, carcass? You would tremble even more if you knew where I was taking you," Turenne mumbled to himself in the heat of the battle. [Henri de la Tour d'Auvergne, Viscount of Turenne (1611–1675), eminent French military commander. The citation is found in Nietzsche's *The Gay Science* (1882).] Fortitude involves a certain fear which is *overcome*, thus made capable of being surmounted in the one who experiences and overcomes it. He does not shrink from the object of his fear and its challenge, nor does he dismiss the great difficulty still before him. Fortitude similarly includes audacity *under restraint*, which does not blindly thrust him into danger. Fortitude is not a happy medium between fear and daring, nor a more or less balanced combination of them, *on their level*. It is placed *on a higher level*, where it verifies the reality of their object. Fortitude does not give in to audacity, which means that it does not disregard the aggressive reaction it prompts, but overcomes it, that is to say, fortitude recognizes the enormous difficulty involved and the surfeit of appropriate effort required to prevail. It *informs* fear

St. Thomas, following Aristotle, concludes from this that fortitude is essentially concerned with the greatest danger a man can face, which affects him precisely at the very point where he exists as man: at the union of soul and body, that is, the peril of death. No doubt, the philosophers add, fortitude is also necessary in the face of lesser dangers, but only in a certain respect (*secundum quid*). The proof they provide is simple: the term *fortitude* must be reserved for the virtue that binds the human will to the good of practical reason, "because he who is capable of standing firm against a greater evil will also stand firm against a lesser one, but not vice versa. It is, in fact, essential to virtue that it be equal to its object even in extreme circumstances. Now, the most terrible of bodily evils is death, which takes away all bodily goods.... The virtue of fortitude, therefore, concerns the fear of the dangers of death" (*timores periculorum mortis*).[3]

This applies to fortitude in the face of death. Fortitude, for the man practicing this virtue, essentially

and daring, like form informs matter. It *determines* their quality and quantity, assesses and evaluates them, and sets boundaries for them. As their regulator, it *imposes itself* on them. In the hierarchy, fortitude holds a higher place than fear and audacity. As has often been said, though our three-dimensional vision is weak, it is the *summit* between two slopes opposite each other. Such is the right balance, the golden mean, of virtue, neither too little nor too much. In the first case, there is an inclination towards laxism. In the second, there is implacable brutality. In both, if we are attentive, it is the self which sets itself up as the sole judge of itself and of others; it is the loss of the *objective* end of the virtue of fortitude; it is the cult of subjectivity. Virtue disappears where individualism reigns (with its immediate corollary, collectivism).

[3] *ST*, II-II, q. 123, art. 4, c., and ad 1.

consists in being in a position, through adequate material and moral preparation, to expose himself to death *propter aliquod bonum consequendum*, for the sake of attaining a certain good. And this good, of which death is the direct consequence, is none other, according to both the Philosopher[4] and St. Thomas, than the defense of the fatherland, which is the common good of all citizens engaged in a just war.[5] To be even more precise, "fortitude manifests itself in its highest degree and in its purest essence in sudden dangers of death. To possess this virtue in its fullness, one must have been able to prepare oneself, through long prior meditation, to sacrifice all private goods, and first and foremost, one's own life, for the good of all — which, for every noble soul, outweighs the individual good,"[6] that is, for the common good.

St. Thomas insists on this point. It might seem, he tells us, that the virtue of fortitude revolves around the good of the human person (*circa personam hominis*), around the human being in his subjectivity who must be preserved from threats of death, rather than around the objective realities (*res*) to which man is bound by his nature as a political animal, and to the protection of which he is therefore committed. Nothing could be further from the truth. "Man does not expose his own life to the dangers of death except for the sake of preserving justice" (*Homo non exponit*

---

[4] Aristotle.

[5] *ST*, II-II, q. 123, art. 5.

[6] Loose quote from *ST*, II-II, q. 123, art. 9. See also *Nic. Eth.* III, 6, 1115a.

personam suam mortis periculis nisi propter justitiam conservandam).[7] Furthermore, St. Thomas tells us even more explicitly that "fortitude has a general usefulness, which is to maintain *the entire order of justice.* This is why, as Aristotle remarks, the just and the brave are the most beloved, for they are the most useful in both war and peace."[8]

The proper function of virtue is, in effect, to safeguard men in the good as indicated by reason. Its specific object is the protection, preservation, and guaranteeing of justice,[9] which every social institution, by its very definition, exists to ensure. And the object of justice is not, in the first instance, the good of the individual person, but the common good of unity, the preeminent value in the practical order, the ultimate goal of man, from which justice is inseparable. "Neither death nor anything else that can be inflicted by a mortal man should ever make us fear to the point of forsaking justice."[10]

For St. Thomas, this is a kind of *human* reflex, the *natural* reaction of practical reason, the guide of all our actions, in the face of the evils and dangers that can affect the society of which man is a part and without which he would be nothing: the social good, the good of political virtue[11] — the principle of all others,

---

[7] *ST*, II-II, q. 123, art. 12, ad 3.

[8] *ST*, II-II, q. 123, art. 12, ad 5; Aristotle's *Rhetoric* II, 9.

[9] *ST*, II-II, q. 124, art. 1, c.

[10] *ST*. II-II, q. 126, ad 2.

[11] In the lofty sense of the term, today unbelievably debased: "All of that, everything worthy of contempt, is politics." See *Le Tremplin* (1919) by the French novelist Gustave Guiches (1860–1935).

and which is called justice — is commensurate with human nature (*commensuratum naturae humanae*). Even the pagans endured great suffering rather than betray their fatherland. The human will, therefore, can be directed toward this good without the aid of sanctifying grace, though not without the help of God, who is the source of every inclination toward the good.[12] This is like an organ of the body which "willingly" sacrifices itself for the preservation of the whole of which it is a part. This prompt commitment to the good of the whole is in the manner of the first principle of the practical order, a self-evident principle. As soon as man applies his practical reason, which is naturally oriented toward the good, to his actions and directs his attention to the good, he perceives with irrefutable certainty that without his collaboration in achieving the common good of unity and without his contribution, however small, to the benefits of the civilization and society in which he lives, he is incapable of living as a man.

In the eras when Aristotle and St. Thomas pointed out this common-sense truth, society was not yet *internally* shaken by the conscious or unconscious nihilism cultivated by its members, a nihilism that always consists in the subordination, by every means imaginable, of the common good to private interest, and of the basic requirements of social life to the claims and so-called rights of the human person. In those former ages, the foundations of societal life remained

[12] *ST*, II-II, q. 136, art. 3, ad 2.

solid: only its summit, political power, swayed under
the pressure of rival factions that sought to seize it,
never, however, with the intention of replacing society
itself with *another one*, artificially constructed, for
their own benefit. Thus, society, the homeland, was
only attacked *from without*, by the *foreigner*, by one
who, not belonging to the besieged society, sought to
destroy it in order to annex its members, in whole or
in part, to his own society.

It is a fact confirmed by history that nations prior
to the sixteenth century feared only other nations, and
that the civil wars that sometimes tore them apart
were wars triggered by personal ambitions for power.
The most typical example is that of the civil wars
that raged under the Roman Republic and Empire.
Never were the Republic or the Empire contested as
such. The same is true of the numerous revolts that
broke out in the Middle Ages. We have to wait until
the Reformation to see religious civil wars evolve into
political civil wars, provoked by the human person
removed from his social context and pursuing nothing
but the goal of establishing paradise on earth.

It was then that the fear of the external enemy was
the most important concern. As a result, fortitude
consisted far more in repressing fear than in moderating
audacity, as the former is "more difficult, since danger,
the common object of both audacity and fear, naturally tends to moderate the latter while increasing the
former."[13] Because the virtue of fortitude is essentially

---

[13] *ST*, II-II, q. 123, art. 6, c.

defined by its highest degree, it will be found more in the act of enduring danger by casting out fear than in the act of appropriately moderating audacity. To remain immobile in the midst of danger requires a greater degree of fortitude.

It is only in appearance that the attacker seems to play the role of the stronger, for the one who resists him must possess far greater strength to repel the assault: the peril he faces is imminent, whereas it appears more remote to his adversary, who envisions himself as the victor. Moreover, "to stand firm requires a long period of time, whereas an attack is often the result of an instantaneous impulse."[14] Now, it is harder to hold firm amid danger for a long time than to throw oneself headlong into a difficult undertaking. The one who endures the assault experiences only a superficial fear, despite having real reasons to be afraid, whereas the one who attacks has no reasons for fear, or very few; otherwise, he would not go on the offensive, and would go from being bold to fearful.[15]

While the principal act of fortitude is to resist, one must not conclude that it involves *only* defense. A certain modern liberalism, if not a particular brand of Christianity inspired by it to the point of intoxication, encourages this misconception. Enduring the evils that afflict us does not, *in itself*, constitute the exercise of

[14] Ibid., ad 1 and 3.
[15] See the text referenced in the above footnote. In his discussion of the virtue of fortitude, St. Thomas holds both that that one who endures feels the presence of danger (ad 1), and that he does not fear (ad 3).

the *virtue* of fortitude. We must also have reasons for
doing so. These reasons are determinative, and they
are what gives fortitude the strength to endure trials.
It is because the soul clings to a reality higher than
itself (a reality that it perceives, through its practical
intelligence, as its *proper* end: either the common
good of the polity or the universal good, which is
God) that it is able to resist. Without an understanding of this, the soul would never be able to eliminate
fear, since the very fear that overwhelms it prevents it
from having recourse to the opposite passion, audacity. It can only resist fear through reason. To endure
evil through *passive* acceptance is neither human nor
Christian. Endurance implies powerful action on the
part of the soul, a robust understanding of the good
that must be accomplished despite everything, and an
ardent desire to attain it, even at the cost of physical
suffering and death,[16] without the least romanticism,
because reason demands it.

From this, it follows that the virtue of fortitude,
though primarily one of resistance, secondarily but
necessarily involves attacks. A certain quite modern
tolerance, covertly complicit, or else linked to hypocrisy derived from a pseudo-Christianity, inclines us to
forget this. On the contrary, it must be asserted that
if it is possible to attack without resisting evil, every
act of resistance necessarily entails a reaction against
evil, and consequently, an attack. If an organism resists
microbes, it also seeks to eliminate them. This is why,

---

[16] Cf. Joseph Pieper, *The Four Cardinal Virtues* (Notre Dame,
IN: University of Notre Dame Press, 1966).

if fortitude employs reason alone in its initial act of resistance, it must, as far as possible, in its second act, achieve victory over evil in order to attain the good, the highest form of which is, let us tirelessly repeat, the common good.

To this end, which is truly its objective, as it is for all virtues, fortitude has recourse to something, according to the realist philosophy of the Master[17] of those who know or who at least strive to know, that "moderates" disapprove of: *anger*. Anger is privileged among all the passions that moral virtues use in moderation, man as a rational animal being an indivisible unity, since anger alone allows fortitude to *effectively* attain its good.

Anger, or a reaction against that which causes suffering, is, as Aristotle says, the most natural source of fortitude, and if the fortitude that derives from it is deliberate and ordered to a good end, it becomes a true virtue.[18] Indeed, anger contains within itself nearly all the passions, not as their genus in relation to species, nor as their cause in relation to effects, but as their outcome.[19] Many passions culminate in anger when they are frustrated. In this sense, reason, which governs and evaluates anger in view of the good — whose highest form, the condition of all others, and found within them, is the common good — directs nearly all the passions towards its own proper end: the establishment of justice through the virtue of

[17] Aristotle.
[18] *ST*, II-II, q. 123, art. 10, ad 3 and *Nic. Eth.*, III, 8, 1117a.
[19] *ST*, I-II, q. 46, art. 1

fortitude, for which anger becomes the appropriate means of assistance.

"Anger is the help of the strong," writes Aristotle[20]; its energy serves as a support for the firm, constant will to render to each his due, which defines justice. Without anger, informed by reason, there can be neither justice nor a penalty for injustice. St. Thomas dares to write, "Anger desires something bad as a means of just retribution. Consequently, anger is directed to those with respect to whom there is justice or injustice. Retribution pertains to justice, and inflicting harm pertains to injustice. Thus, both from the standpoint of cause, that is, the harm inflicted by another, and from the standpoint of the retribution sought by the person who is angry, anger concerns those to whom we are connected by justice or injustice."[21]

We have completely lost this sense of righteous anger as indispensable to the virtue of fortitude and to the *realization* of justice. To us moderns, anger is nothing more than a rebellion against the fate dealt to us personally or to those whom we, in our imagination, identify with our own selves. It then erupts in violence. Leaving no doubt, St. Thomas assures us that "the motive of a man's anger is always something that has been done to himself."[22] Anger is a reaction to an obstacle which, in the form of an insult or offense, confronts us in our subjectivity, and which we take as an injustice done to us personally, or to

[20] The source of this quote could not be identified.
[21] *ST*, I-II, q. 46, art. 7, c.
[22] *ST*, I-II, q. 47, art. 1, c.

others grouped together as a sort of collective person with whom we are conflated. The examples of this in current politics are innumerable.

But righteous anger, which fuels fortitude, has nothing subjective about it, except its relationship to the initial cause, the reaction which sets it in motion. Yet, in matters of action, it is not the initial cause that governs, but the *final cause*: the good. It is not so much the personal injury that we suffer that sets righteous anger in motion, but rather the obstacle pitted against the *objective* good, against the *common* good, the pursuit of which is inscribed in the very nature of man — and in his nature elevated to the supernatural.

Just as fortitude, which, as we have said with St. Thomas, "has a general utility, which is to safeguard *the entire order of justice, (totum justitiae ordinem),*"[23] so too righteous anger that serves fortitude has as its end the full restoration of this order. This can only be achieved if practical reason directs it towards its proper end: the common good, the origin of all others. Such was the righteous anger of Christ, who drove the merchants from the Temple with a whip in order to purify the divine sanctuary. Such was human justice, which, until recently, punished the perpetrator of premeditated murder against a member of society with the death penalty, in order to restore the social order, which had been disrupted by the presence of an element unworthy of being part of the whole.

[23] *ST*, II-II, q. 123, art. 12, ad 5.

From all that has been said, it follows that fortitude
is intimately linked with justice and with the common
good, which is its end. One may even say that it is
inseparable from them. St. Thomas does not even separate the supernatural order from the natural order in
this regard. *Martyrdom* is, for him, an act of human
fortitude elevated by grace. There is, therefore, only a
single virtue of fortitude, but it is placed, according
to the two ends it serves, on two different levels, one
higher than the other: "In the act of fortitude, two
things must be considered: the good[24] in which the
brave man is confirmed, and which is the end of
fortitude; and the firmness with which he withstands
everything that would seek to keep him from this
good, which constitutes the very essence of fortitude.
Now, just as natural fortitude strengthens a man with
regard to *human justice*, for the preservation of which
he braves the danger of death, supernatural fortitude
strengthens a man with regard to '*the justice of God,
through faith in Jesus Christ*' (Rom. 3:22). Faith, to
which one remains steadfast, is therefore the end of

[24] In the commentary which accompanies his translation of
Somme théologique, La force (Paris, 1949), Father Jean-Dominique
Folghera considers that under the term "the good" are included
"this virtue [fortitude] and duty." We hold, on the contrary, that
all virtues are included inasmuch as they are related, according to
St. Thomas, to the virtue of justice and to the duty of defending
the fatherland which is the good of all and from which all human
goods are in fact derived. This is indeed the loftiest of human
goods — the natural common good — which makes man steadfast
to the highest degree, as the end communicates its power to the
agent who is striving towards it. *Bonum reipublicae est praecip-
ium inter bona humana* [The good of the republic is paramount
among human goods] (*ST*, II-II, q. 124, art. 5, ad 3).

the act of martyrdom; fortitude is the *habitus* that produces this act."[25]

Undoubtedly it is only endurance, the principal act of fortitude, that constitutes the essence of martyrdom, with the exclusion of attack, which is its secondary act.[26] But St. Thomas in no way excludes the use of offensive force, armed with righteous anger, in the defense of the faith, for example, against infidels or heretics. In keeping with the entire tradition of the Church, he delegates this task to the secular arm. To Peter, representing bishops and clerics, it is said in the Gospel of Matthew: "Put your sword back into its sheath" [26:52]. The clergy may call the faithful to arms, but they are forbidden by ecclesiastical law and custom from participating in battle with weapons in hand. "No one serving in the army of God gets entangled in worldly affairs."[27] In this sense, the virtue of fortitude, as they[28] demonstrate in its secondary aspect, already surpasses its primary aspect, endurance. If the Church leaves infidels and heretics to the secular arm, it is by virtue of the subordination of human government, which possesses the means of enforcement, to divine government. Thus, it follows that if the means of enforcement, equipped with the coercive power of civil law, proves weak or even disappears entirely, as in modern times, then the harm inflicted upon the kingdom of God will be great. If

[25] *ST*, II-II, q. 124, art. 2, ad 1.
[26] Ibid., ad 3.
[27] An adaptation of 2 Tim. 2:4. See also *ST*, II-II, q. 40, art. 2.
[28] Presumably De Corte is referring here to secular forces.

divine fortitude no longer strengthens failing human fortitude, the damage suffered in earthly society will be no less considerable.

Liberalism, which abhors the virtue of fortitude, and religious liberalism, which tolerates the worst transgressions of divine law, always go hand in hand. We must have the courage to repeat it with St. Thomas: "Faith is the reign of God in minds. If there are any who presume to alter it while remaining within it, as heretics do, or who leave it ostentatiously, as apostates do, it is evident that the society of the faithful, of which they are a part, has both the right and the duty to take action against such people — whether to recall them to order, or even to force them back into it, or at the very least, to prevent them from disturbing it."[29]

How could the virtue of fortitude, in its secondary aspect, still exist in the Church and civil society when its primary function of resisting all forms of evil has been completely, or almost completely, obscured in people's minds, even among those who ought to possess it in an eminent degree?

"No more anathemas!" cried John XXIII the Good at the opening of Vatican II. Meanwhile, public opinion polls reveal that 57 percent of the French are not willing to die for their country, while at the same

[29] See *ST*, II-II, q. 10, art. 8, c, and q. 11, art.3. See also note 66, p. 284 in *Somme théologique, La foi* by Father A. Bernard, OP (Paris, 1963): "More than one of us will be surprised at the conclusion of St. Thomas, articulated with great confidence. However, he speaks the truth, which is no longer within our reach."

time, one in two young people aged 18 to 24 would refuse to respond to a mobilization order.

The virtue of fortitude is vanishing before our eyes, giving way to violence, coercion, and a web of pseudo-social obligations and demands, the totality of which — whether on an individual or collective level, whether sporadic or long-lasting — produces, in the dis-society born from a lack of fortitude, a vague fear, an undefined apprehension, an obscure anxiety. These are most often concealed beneath an uninterrupted pursuit of pleasure that uproots man even further from his human context. And yet, when this latent unease is suddenly brought to light, terror, dread, and panic result. The contemporary man is swept between two extremes, fear and audacity, caught in an endless oscillation between inertia, passivity, and stagnation on one hand, and restlessness, turmoil, and innova-tion at all costs on the other. In short, he is carried towards *permanent revolution*, like a colloid, a gelat-inous mass that simultaneously combines stagnation and frenzy. Permanent chaos and constant instability, such is the condition of modern man deprived of the virtue of fortitude.

III

THE ELIMINATION OF
THE VIRTUE OF FORTITUDE
IN TODAY'S WORLD

THUS TO PROPERLY GRASP the vices opposed to fortitude today, one must look beyond fear and audacity. When St. Thomas enumerates them— fear, the absence of fear, and audacity—he is speaking within the context of a stable, well-ordered society, one whose foundation (general justice) remains unshaken.[1] The medieval state knew nothing of individualism, personalism, or the cult of the self. Nevertheless, St. Thomas foresaw with great acuity the disorders of modernity. He understood that "order requires the submission of the appetitive faculty to the governance of reason," specifically, to practical reason directed towards the common good. He also recognized that "in human acts, *disorder* is a sin."[2] He knew that "fear always proceeds from love, for one only fears that which opposes what one loves" and that "fear disordered by disordered love is opposed

---

[1] *ST*, II-II, q. 125, art. 1, 2, and 3.
[2] Ibid., art. 1.

to fortitude," *which always has the same object*, which is, let us repeat, the common good of the fatherland or of the natural and semi-natural communities to which destiny and vocation attach us.[3]

St. Thomas knew that to yield to the supreme fear of a death that should be accepted so that society may survive beyond the fleeting existence of the individual is disordered, and is the quintessential sin against fortitude. To commit this sin is to choose the self, to prioritize one's private good over the general good. "Neither death nor anything else that can afflict a mortal man should be feared to the point of causing us to renounce justice."[4] One may certainly experience fear, but one has the duty to overcome it.

For other reasons which again stem from a disordered appetitive faculty that withdraws from the order of practical reason and the common good, the same applies to the absence of fear and to audacity. Both are sins against fortitude. Yet, audacity is not always a lack of fear! Aristotle observed that the bold, full of ardor when there is nothing to fear, do not know how to endure *true* danger.[5] In this case, they too are cowards who sin against the virtue of fortitude and who refuse to defend the common good effectively.

From this, one sees clearly that the sin most directly opposed to the virtue of fortitude can ultimately be reduced to a form of rebellion against the common good, and that this rebellion, in the end, is nothing

[3] Ibid., art. 2, c.
[4] Ibid., q. 126, art. 1, ad 2.
[5] See *Nic. Eth.*, III, 7.

other than the exaltation of the self and its individual good. If St. Thomas does not explicitly speak of this, it is because the society of his time was not yet corroded by individual and collective selfishness. However, the principles of his analysis are eternal and are a beacon of light for all eras. Once selfishness arises and man withdraws into himself, pursuing only his own individual good while abandoning the common good, disorder reaches its highest level and manifests itself in its most characteristic sin: The absence of fear results "from the fact that man thinks it is impossible for him to be afflicted by evils opposed to the goods he loves. This belief may stem from pride, which leads one to overestimate oneself and to despise others — *ex superbia animi de se praesumentis et alios contemnentis.*" Ruthlessness, equally narrow-minded, believes that the self comes before everything. Thus, St. Thomas is right to place arrogance and stupidity on the same level.[6] Both alienate the man they overpower from true social life.

Thus, through the Thomistic diagnosis of the vices opposed to the virtue of fortitude, one can easily identify their origin and how they become more widespread: the self, which sets itself up as the ultimate end of human life, both natural and supernatural; the "rights of man", understood in the full breadth of their destructive subjectivity; and a lack of patience in attaining the end and the common good, to which man is subject by his status as a political animal.

---

[6] *ST*, II-II, q. 126, art. 1, c.

By following this trajectory, it is immediately apparent that the virtue of fortitude, in order to be victorious, must not only resist the fear of physical death or unrestrained, animal-like audacity, which, in the form of pride, pervades the disoriented soul. It must also confront a vague widespread unease, an anxiety that explodes into violence — either sporadically or pervasively — as a kind of remedy for inadequacy, or even cowardice, which is its underlying cause.

The ancient city-states and medieval societies experienced revolts, peasant uprisings, popular insurrections, and numerous wars among themselves. However, they were entirely ignorant of revolution as a strategic phenomenon and the relentless subversion that now works to dismantle modern society and transform it into a dis-society, manifesting itself at various levels, from conflicts between political parties to class struggle.

The persecution faced by Christians today no longer confronts them with a tragic choice: abjuration of their faith or death. Rather, it is the very foundations of the social order, both natural and supernatural, that are now crumbling, under both external and internal pressures. Society and the Church alike are threatened with self-destruction, whether through the passive acceptance of the infiltration of disorder in their midst or through active complicity with it.

For two or three centuries now, our contemporaries have sought to construct a new society, one built artificially from the ground up, dismissing both the nature of man as a political animal and the experience of the past. Similarly, today's clerics aspire to build a new Church. As Paul VI once proclaimed, in a kind of ecstasy: "The word *innovation*, simple, widely used, congenial to modern man.... has been given to us as a command, as a program."[7] Yet St. Thomas assures us that *the love of novelties, which men are greatly prone to wonder at, is the direct effect of vainglory,*[8] with which the self enhaloes itself.

Martyrdom is no longer, for the vast majority of Christians today, a physical ordeal. *It is spiritual. It involves an attack on practical reason, abstracting it from the common good of unity, which is necessary for every society. Faith in the one, holy, Catholic, and apostolic Church is attacked. Christians, and those who are no longer Christian or have yet to become so, are confronted by a denial of the principles upon which human society and the society of the faithful are founded.*

The virtue of fortitude is all the more indispensable for our contemporaries because the state of dis-society in which they have been immersed for several generations has *weakened* them. No one is more weak and powerless than the isolated individual, addicted to the drug of individualism and personalism. Yet his aggregation with others does not restore the strength he lacks—on the contrary! A grouping together of weaknesses, far from resulting in strength, only produces a formless mass, which can be molded into any shape by its subversive leaders. This is precisely

[7] General audience, July 2, 1969.
[8] *ST*, II-II, art. 132, q. 5, c.

what man and the Christian must resist through the virtue of fortitude.

For the extent to which a human being renounces his nature as a political animal ordered to the common good is the extent to which he separates himself from his fellow men. A part that withdraws from the whole is no longer a part. No language can give it a name, but rather, it becomes nothing more than an individual, an anonymous person, featureless, devoid of any distinct character. Such a man is pure potentiality, as the Philosopher would say, incapable of actualizing himself, receiving his mode of being and acting only from external influences. He is shaped by the manipulative techniques employed by those who control the anonymous mass in which he is engulfed.

An attack on the masses, whether through propaganda or advertising, is a phenomenon of dis-society. It arises from the profound weakness of man's political *nature*, a nature compromised by individualism and personalism, leaving him almost entirely defenseless against the ills that afflict him. Such a social invalid cannot help but be anxious, even physically so, given the connection between mind and body. He is "uncomfortable in his own skin," as modern jargon puts it, because his nature no longer complies with the norms that govern it and direct it towards its end.

The ploy of the violent agent—and the trap he sets, into which he himself falls when he goes from a state of latent anxiety to excited elation—is to introduce into this weakened soul artificial ways of functioning

that substitute for his now-fluid nature. These give
him the *illusion* of being "comfortable in his own
skin," enclosed within his compartmentalized indi-
viduality, yet without any *real* relationship with other
people in the concrete reality of daily life.

Because virtue is always determined by specific
circumstances — by place, time, opportunity, and its
concrete manifestation in the thousand and one contingencies of life where it is *actually practiced* — it
is not surprising that fortitude is not only directed
to keeping the human will aligned with the common good by enabling it to resist the great perils
that might assail it, especially resisting the danger
of death from war, bravely fighting off the assaults
coming from within societies in which man finds
himself, and defending the fatherland from external
attacks. Today, the domain of fortitude has expanded
far beyond these traditional spheres. For it is one thing
to face physical death in battle against an adversary
who seeks only to destroy his opponent's life or to
subjugate him or a particular polity, as was the case in
past centuries, when there was no threat to the very
nature of the individual or collective mind. But it is
quite another thing to be confronted with a system
of external and internal pressures that prevent human
knowledge and will from attaining to the realities for
which they were made. These pressures target the
social nature of man, as it flourishes in the natural
and semi-natural communities where it reaches its full
development, and attempt to destroy it by means that
range from insinuating and intimidating propaganda

to brutal terror, and to re-create it in the cast of a prefabricated ideology, supposedly generating a "new man" and a "new society." This has been underway for the past two or three centuries.

If to this violence, latent or open, which we experience in the dis-society of today, we add the stratagem which is openly implemented within the Catholic Church — a maneuver aimed primarily at turning souls from the worship of God to the worship of Man, capitalized — the situation becomes even more revealing. "All things on earth should be related to man as their source and crown," boldly decrees Vatican II.[9] It is no longer only man's natural common good that is explicitly challenged, but his supernatural common good as well. What is now at stake is not merely his physical life, but his nature as a political animal and his personal redemption.

Stripped of their evangelical goal, man can only direct his spiritual energies towards one *concrete* end: the Self. The accelerated protestantization of Catholicism (and of its clergy, with the hierarchy deprived of the virtue of fortitude) has no other origin. This redirection, inspired by nihilism, in which the self becomes its own victim (for the self is nothing without its natural and supernatural social relationships), is undermining the bulwarks of both the state and the Church. History offers no precedent for this.

[9] *Gaudium et Spes*, 12. Here follows the full passage: "According to the almost unanimous opinion of believers and unbelievers alike, all things on earth should be related to man as their center and crown." [Translation from the Vatican website.]

If this analysis is correct, *then the virtue of forti-tude — and its effective application in every domain: intellectual, moral, social and secular — now takes on unprecedented importance, in both of its characteristic roles, resistance and attack.* In the traditional ranking of the cardinal virtues, fortitude is normally placed immediately after prudence and justice, and before temperance. But now under the influence of justice, which fortitude then directs, and through the selection of prudential means to reach its goal, which it sharply defines, fortitude takes its place *at the top.*

St. Thomas foresaw this when he assigned to forti-tude, in addition its own end which we have spoken of, an unquestionably universal function: the dis-tinguishing mark of all true virtues is resolute stead-fastness, and when fortitude becomes less robust, all virtues are indeed weakened.[10] A quick look at the moral, political, and social condition of humanity today is enough to confirm this: the refusal to trace this decline back to its *cause*, blindness to its conse-quences, and the use of subterfuge or violence in an effort to remedy it are all obvious.

It is for this reason that fortitude must accompany all virtues. Where fortitude is lacking, we find taking root and running rampant: moral and political decay, religious indifference, and the desperate pursuit of pleasure for its own sake.[11]

[10] See *ST*, II-II, q. 123 art. 2, c.

[11] Let us recall that in Thomistic Aristotelianism, pleasure is by no means prohibited, since it accompanies the practice of virtue, which brings happiness, "like the bloom given to youth." [See

Fortitude is eminently the friend of prudence in the order of means. We must insist on this point, for we too often tend to transpose human *action* to the theoretical level, where it dissolves into concepts that are intellectually satisfying but lose their specific connection with reality *in actu exercito*.[12] The end of action is not a given from the outset, an idea for the mind to contemplate. Rather, it is a good *to be realized*. By what means? By a series of appropriate means, which prudence organizes, sets in motion, and directs. There is a force in prudence that commands, that knows (because it is so empowered) that it will, *ut in pluribus*,[13] almost always reach its goal, despite the contingencies that affect all human action. As the admirable Bossuet expresses it, with forceful words that are also a call to action: "True prudence is not merely analytical; it is also incisive and resolute."[14] For if prudence, according to this same theologian, has the task of "putting everything in order," this order does not consist solely in the ordering and arrangement of things, nor in "the conformity of the means to the end" that the intellect elaborates *ad intra*[15] and keeps internalized. Rather, order also requires a command (*imperium*) that orders the will to take action. *This*

Nic. Eth., I, 4.] Its radiance spills over from the soul to the body. Man is irreducibly a composite being, neither angel nor beast.

[12] In actual action, when put into practice.

[13] In most cases.

[14] "Quatrième sermon pour le dimanche des rameaux, sur la justice" in *Oeuvres complètes de Bossuet*, vol. IX, Paris, 1862. Jacques-Bénigne Bossuet (1627–1704), French bishop and theologian renowned for his homilies.

[15] Within itself.

presupposes that kind of fortitude, which as we have seen does not consist today in standing firm in physical peril, but in preserving the essence of man, above all his nature as a "political animal" on both the natural and supernatural levels, against the ever-increasing dangers that threaten the existence of this nature, and in coun-terattacking the enemies swarming around it which seek to subjugate and reshape it, in order to annihilate it. [16]

Thus, one may rightly affirm that prudence itself arises, as from its very source, from the virtue of forti-tude, which resists both external and internal attacks and successfully eliminates the obstacles that hinder the fulfillment of human nature and the support offered by divine grace. In both civil society and the Church, fortitude is the guardian of the political animal whose integration into social existence is itself the end of all moral actions, governed by prudence and directed by the imperatives of morality. Thus, St. Ambrose declares that fortitude is the most excellent of all virtues: *est for-titudo velut ceteris excelsior*). [17] One need only observe the consequences that follow, both for human nature and for the highest goods to which it is ordered, when fortitude is absent and its opposite prevails: *weakness*.

Cardinal de Retz with incomparable perspicac-ity observed this in the midst of the turmoil of the Fronde [18]: "*The effects of weakness are unimaginable,*

[16] We have used here revised text from our study "La vertu de force contre la violence révolutionnaire" in the *Actes du congrès de Lausanne*, VI, April–May 1972, Paris.

[17] Fortitude is higher than the rest (*De Officiis* I).

[18] Jean François Paul de Gondi de Retz (1613–1679), writer and political activist, and, later, archbishop of Paris. The Fronde was

and I maintain that they are more astonishing than those of the most violent passions." Let us recall here that all human passions originate, psychologically and, above all, ontologically, from two central faculties: the irascible appetite, whose object is the *arduum*, the difficult good to be attained and the painful evil to be avoided, and the concupiscible appetite, whose object is the good to be obtained. Both are expressions of the sensitive appetite, which is obviously rooted in the body, which gives them a distinctive character varying from one person to the next; in order to be oriented to what is objective, the subjective energy of the appetites must attain a final end that is *truly* the end of man, either on the natural level or as elevated and directed by grace to the God of revelation.

How could we achieve this without prudence and fortitude? Temperance also requires both virtues in order to properly regulate the concupiscible appetite.[19] Even at the mere level of physical activity, such as walking, eating, or drinking, etc., we know that some goods are difficult to attain ("By the sweat of your brow you shall eat" [Genesis 3:19].) Similarly, some evils must be avoided (do not do this, do not do that). To accomplish even the smallest good, one must conquer oneself. The first movement of nature prompts us to do this, but what about the second? It takes self-mastery to resist the attraction of what Hesiod

a series of civil wars in France in the mid-seventeenth century in which nobles and commoners resisted the centralizing actions of the monarchy, and to which the cardinal lent his support. The citation is from his *Mémoires* (1717).

[19] See *Temperance*, forthcoming from Arouca Press.

called a "beautiful evil."[20] For an evil that did not present itself in the guise of a good would immediately repel us. One must also overcome opposition from external forces, or, at least, resist them.

The education of man does not consist in "creativity," as foolish people say today. It involves the strength to say *no* to the temptation to surrender to weakness — to that withdrawal into a cautious subjective state that, while dissembling, comforts itself with all kinds of excuses — and to the delightful evils that besiege us. Every *yes* to a good begins with a *no*, for adults as well as for children, who would not survive long without the restraining power exercised by their parents or educators. This strength to say no to weakness is all the more necessary today, because modern individualism, personalism, subjectivism, "humanism," and immanentism, by rejecting the transcendence of the *true* good, whether social or religious, have made men susceptible to utopias, myths, ideological propaganda, and deceitful advertising.

Where the first movement of life, which is to overcome death, is no longer supported by practical reason and by the fortitude necessary for it to take hold, it is replaced by the dynamism of the imagination — which constructs anything at all, any kind of society, any kind of religion, even an atheistic one, rather than have man confront the unimaginable void of nothingness. Where authority, the guardian of

[20] The ancient Greek poet (fl. c. 700 BC) in his poem *Theogony* so described Pandora, whose physical beauty masked the evil she brought into the world.

the common good in the state and in the Church, erodes, falters, or abdicates at every turn, then the will to power of laity and clerics is unleashed and works relentlessly to instill in those who still exercise the virtue of fortitude and resist the subversion of all values a *guilty conscience* about their unyielding frame of mind, which is revealed in their actions.

There are few realities (or concepts) more ambiguous than *conscience*, as the moderns understand it. For them, it has become the principle faculty of moral and political life which governs all human activities. St. Thomas is far more reserved on this matter. For him, conscience is understood in an entirely different sense, a radically different one. Conscience is neither a faculty nor a *habitus*, but simply an act of the intellect that applies itself to an action we carry out.[21] Sometimes it is synonymous with synderesis,[22] that "spark" (*scintilla*) of the soul, that humble (*modica*) intuition by which every human being, no matter how low his moral level, comprehends the fundamental principles of human action. The first principle, as we know, is that "One must do good and avoid evil." Synderesis is like the eye of an eagle (*aquila*). It is a kind of natural light that illuminates our actions and points out to us their proper end.[23] It is the supreme law that governs our acts, and it is never obliterated — not even in the greatest criminal or sinner. Reason, as the

---

[21] *ST*, I, q. 79, art. 13, c. and I-II, q. 19, art. 5, c.
[22] The innate ability to understand the first principles of morality, the difference between right and wrong.
[23] *ST*, I, q, 79, art. 12, c; *De Veritate*, q. 16, art. 1, c and ad 9; *Commentary on the Sentences*, II, d. 24, q. 2, art. 3.

principle of human action, never entirely disappears in man, except in cases of insanity, but in that case there is no longer any human act at all.

However, practical reason has as its first principle man's ultimate end, and the ultimate end of human life is happiness or beatitude, man's objective good. For man is an animal who lives in society. "For every part is ordered to the whole as the imperfect is ordered to the perfect. The individual human being is part of a perfect community.[24] *It is thus necessary for the law to be directly oriented towards communal happiness.* This is why the Philosopher, when speaking of laws and their definition, always mentions their orientation towards communal happiness, for he says that we call those legal provisions just that establish and preserve happiness and all that contributes to it in the body politic. Indeed, the perfect society is the state . . . The law only takes on its full meaning when it is oriented towards the common good (*ad bonum commune*). Any other precept (*omnis lex*) that addresses a particular act only acquires the value of law insofar as it is ordered to this common good."[25] Thus, the common good subjects the human individual to an *objective end*, which is the law natural to him, imposed upon him by his very nature as a political animal, which he cannot resist, no matter what he does.

[24] In the last two sentences, "imperfect" and "perfect" can be translated "incomplete" and complete."

[25] *ST*, I-II, q. 90, art. 2 and 3; see also q. 91 art. 5; q. 92, art. 1; q. 93, art. 1, ad 1; q. 95, art. 3 and 4; q. 96. art. 1, 3, 4, and 6; q. 97, art. 1; q. 100, art. 2; II-II, q. 58, art. 5; *Nic. Eth.* V, 1; Aquinas's *Commentary on Aristotle's Politics*, I, 1.

Thus, we can affirm without the slightest risk of error that synderesis, or the *habitus* of the first principles of human acts, is essentially directed to the objective common good of the state, in the natural order, and to God, in the supernatural order. The word "conscience," which is sometimes (*quandoque*) used in place of synderesis, can therefore only refer to a conscience which is objective.

However, since conscience is also subjective, it can be directed to "objects" that appropriate this designation, mere products of individual consciousness, which is their sole principle and their sole end. This explains why St. Thomas rarely uses this highly ambiguous term, which plays only a very minor role in his masterwork, the *Summa Theologiae*.[26] Unlike modern thinkers, who enthusiastically exalt the individual "conscience" — "Conscience! conscience! Immortal and celestial voice!"[27] — and the opposite of modern scholastics, who are fascinated by a philosophy entirely foreign to the one they pretend to profess, having replaced the traditional treatises on prudence with the labyrinthine *Tractatus de conscientia*,[28] influenced by a Protestantized or secularized Christianity, St. Thomas holds that the notion of conscience casts on human acts only a light based on abstractions. It has nothing to do with carrying out actions, as

---

[26] See *De Veritate*, 17, 2, where St. Thomas affirms that the conscience can fall into error — which is all too evident! — but that synderesis cannot err.

[27] From Rousseau's *Émile* (1762).

[28] Several treatises on conscience have appeared in modern times.

widespread experience confirms. Prudence, by contrast, is an *objective, reality-oriented* virtue, a virtue of *action that exercises control and is based on the common good*. "The judgment of conscience consists simply in knowledge" (*judicium conscientiæ consistit in pura cognitione*), which, as such, far from inciting action, is reduced to endless speculation, and by its absence of practical objectivity engenders a debilitating anxiety in souls.[29] When introduced into morality and politics, the subjectivist concept of conscience paralyzes action. In order to act, man must then have recourse to the nebulous forces of instinct and sentiment, to the exclusion of the practical intellect.

This digression was necessary to understand why the subjective conscience has made modern man incapable of resisting, through virtuous acts of fortitude, the great threats to which he is subjected in today's dissociety, since he is imprisoned within his individual or collective self and limited to the exclusive pursuit of his own private good. This digression was also necessary to perceive that the distortion of justice and the enormous degradation it has undergone in our time are due to the same root cause: the weakness of modern man and his tendency to resort to animal violence, masked under abstract ideologies, powerless in themselves, as a way to escape from the chaos into which he is descending.

The virtue of fortitude is intimately connected with the virtue of justice, though not with the "justice" of

---

[29] *De Veritate.* q. 17, art. 1, ad 4. See the fine pages Father Thomas Deman, OP dedicated to this problem in *Traité de la prudence, Somme théologique* (Paris, 1949).

today, the mere mention of which stuns and stupefies us. Rather, fortitude is linked to the form of justice concerned with the common good, which is called general or legal justice. This point must be constantly reaffirmed: Justice consists in rendering to each his due, what is due him *as a priority*, without which no other form of justice can exist. This is *life in society*, in accordance with the norms of the natural law and the directives of practical reason, that allow man to be what he is by nature in a concrete and effective way: a political animal,[30] bound to collaborate, across space and time, with contemporary and future generations, so that each individual may share in what society has to offer, the religious, moral, artistic, scientific and technical contributions of all members to the common good. This consequence of general justice for the citizens of the state is called *distributive justice*.

Here, whether we speak of justice as "mother" or justice as "daughter," we are in the concrete realm of action. It is an undeniable fact that, unlike the abstract sphere of speculative thought, where man fulfills his definition as a rational animal and where, in this sense, all men are equal, *men are radically unequal in the field of action*, not only in a quantitative sense but also with regard to qualitative nature of their activities. Nature is the privileged domain of natural inequalities arising from birth, natural dispositions, and the infinite variety of gifts bestowed by an inexhaustible Providence on men, who either foster them

---

[30] This does not mean: an animal provided with a ballot of his own, as in universal suffrage in and of itself.

or let them wither away, so that men become even
more dissimilar to each other over time. A saint or
hero is not the equal of a scoundrel in the order of
action, nor is a hardworking father of a family the
equal of a vagrant.

To build a society from such obviously disparate
elements, a unifying *force* is necessary that comman-
deers man's first natural inclinations towards the
social life, makes them fruitful, organizes them, and
aligns them to the supreme good, which men seek but
cannot attain on their own, since most individuals lack
both continuity of purpose and a broad perception
of their common interests. There is no need to add
that original sin, by separating man from himself and
from others, in the brilliant expression of a Church
Father, has further exacerbated this social asthenia.
For this reason, Aristotle and St. Thomas never cease
to praise the man who first built a city.

How can we do this? Through the virtue of fortitude, which gathers around itself collaborators
endowed with this virtue. To render to each his due
in distributive justice is to establish each person within
the social hierarchy, without which no community can
exist, giving him the place where he belongs, according
to the services he has rendered to the common good,
the soul of the polity. *It is impossible for the common
good to come into existence, endure, or be transmitted
without the virtue of fortitude,* "at least among those
responsible for governing."[31] This is why Aristotle

---

[31] *ST*, I-II, q. 92, art. 1, ad 3.

says that *"the virtue of the (true) ruler is identical to that of the good man,"* proportioned to the common good, "but this is not true of any citizen whatever."[32] *And the virtue of the good man, in addition to prudence and justice, lies in the cardinal virtue of fortitude.*

Can we still be sure that this holds true in an era such as ours, where the egalitarian myth holds sway? For this myth is as opposite as possible to the reality of the common good and the virtue of fortitude, which subordinates those at a lower level to those at a higher level in every society that is even remotely ordered, even in dis-societies, where society is changed into a coercive bureaucratic or police state. Perhaps one of the most glaring and least recognized lies of the modern world is its use of the term *social justice* to describe the corpse of true justice.

What our contemporaries understand by social justice is to render to each person, *taken as an individual*, what is due him, putting him on an equal footing with all other members of his group. In modern liberal or totalitarian democracies, all citizens have in the strictest sense an equal vote. They all participate to the same degree, with the same ballot in hand, in the "social" machinery, where they function as identical cogs. It hardly needs to be said that such a "society" is the negation of all true society, since it is, in principle, composed of absolutely identical grains of sand. Each these, as he has politically speaking nothing more or less than the others, can no longer render to each what

---

[32] *Commentary on Aristotle's Politics*, III, 3.

is due him, and, in turn, cannot receive what is due him from others. Such a "society," *without general justice*, is then a society without any justice at all.

Thus, this dis-society is always in search of social justice. Its members, if they can still be called such, have only this one word on their lips, some to defend their remaining non-political rights, their wealth, for example, and others to take those rights away from them. This is how opposing political parties arise, the haves and have-nots,[33] the "right" and the "left," who substitute their members' individual interests for the common good, if perchance it still exists. And in place of general justice, safeguarded by the virtue of fortitude, they establish a pseudo-justice, whose instrument is violence. Then a change of direction in politics follows, a complete about-face. This does not even have to do with politics, except for the use of the term, since there remains no more common good to defend through the virtue of fortitude, only individual goods to be protected or demanded, using all the means that a weak state allows or all those arrogated to itself by the apparatus of the hyperbolic state.

We now understand the quasi-disappearance in the modern era of natural and semi-natural communities:

[33] There are certainly "haves" on the left. In the democratic communist system we indeed find the biggest owners, as Milovan Djilas has irrefutably shown in his book *La nouvelle classe dirigeante* (1957). In the final analysis, the secretary general of the communist party, in the countries where he rules, is a capitalist on a scale never surpassed by any multibillionaire. [Djilas (1911–1995) was a former Yugolav communist official who became disillusioned with communism.]

the family, trades and professions, region and country, even civilization[34] itself; man has neither created these out of nothing nor chosen them. The common good of these communities and the virtue of fortitude are interconnected, and the disappearance of one leads to the disappearance of the other. It is these multiple communities, each with its own particular common good, yet able to complement one another, that receive man at birth and envelop him in their tutelary environment from cradle to grave. However, their continued existence, virtues, and benefits can only be maintained through deliberate human effort. These communities uphold the public common good and are its solid foundations, unshakable as long as man, who is strengthened by all of them, does not surrender to the weakness of dispensing with them; in order to endure, they require fortitude of him. *Nothing is more fragile than this truly human order, or more constantly threatened.* Death constantly lies in wait; death strips man of his goods by taking away the first of them, his existence; death, the greatest of evils, constantly looms over these communities, if the virtue of fortitude, which as we have seen by its nature stands against death, is not there to protect

---

[34] This word has been replaced by culture. Civilizations, as indicated by etymology, are tied to cities and states. [*Cités* in French, from the Latin *civitas*, meaning city, state, or citizen.] Culture implies only the use of the intellectual faculty, universal by definition, which uproots from their environment those who limit themselves to its cultivation. Culture has no concern for practical reason whose end is the respective common good of polities; it "frees" the individual and grants him all his "rights."

them from this threat. The order of the common good is woven out of billions of real relationships, most of them unconscious, that bind men together.

Yet nothing is easier than severing these quasi-organic connections, the lifeblood of the community. *It is enough to proclaim the self.* Nothing more is needed. All it takes is to elevate the individual as both principle and *end* — for in the domain of action, the end is also the principle! — *of the social order.* This is what was done with unparalleled audacity, and, it must be said, stupidity — by some 2500 mitred heads at Vatican II, wholeheartedly endorsed by Paul VI. It is enough to subordinate the general interest to particular interests, whether individual or collective, to weaken the virtue of fortitude. Then, with an inevitable boomerang effect, the reversal of values is accelerated as fortitude falters. Simply put, all it takes is to follow one's *own* inclinations. This tendency is inborn: one can go down the slippery slope at any moment. This happens as soon as one considers natural and semi-natural communities not as revitalizing and invigorating environments, but as shackles that stifle man's "personality."

This also explains why the political order has yielded to the economic order in the hierarchy of values of contemporary humanity, despite all the difficulties caused by this primacy, setbacks that man vainly hopes to eliminate by the augmentation of the means that produced them.

The economic order differs from the political order just as *making* differs from *acting* and material well-being differs from the common good. Its end is strictly individual, the consumer in flesh and blood, with this or that name, the only one capable of utilizing material goods, which are always destined to the individual. Thus, it is only by way of metaphor that we say that France or Belgium consumed, for example, so many tons of butter in 1979. In reality, the French and Belgians obviously consumed it as individuals. A collective entity, devoid of a human body, is incapable of consumption! Moreover, while the domain of politics is governed by general justice, of which distributive justice is an extension, proportioned to the services rendered to society, the domain of economics is governed by *commutative justice*. In the first case, parity presumes that justice is "geometrical," and in the second case, "arithmetical." If you give me "two" of something, I am obliged, according to commutative justice, to give you back "two." But the citizen, regardless of his place in the social hierarchy, receives infinitely more from the actual society to which he belongs, and to whose common good he is dedicated, than anything he could give back, including his life.

In contrast, in a society where economics governs human activity exclusively, the law of arithmetical equality which is sovereign tends to penetrate every other sphere of life, opening the door to universal egalitarianism, bringing in its wake a retinue of claims and demands. An intense struggle ensues, never ending and for a reason, against every kind of inequality inherent in existence, from economic to "cultural," and even to those related to "opportunities," in an effort to eliminate the "accidents" of birth and the gifts bestowed through the caprices of who knows what preposterous deity, which must be removed in turn. This is why Trotsky became famous for predicting, as early as 1921, that the men of the future would surpass in depth and stature the greatest geniuses of the past. What is called "reformed" education is headed in this direction.

From this arises the cult rendered by modern man to Technology, along with Science, which he holds to have no other purpose than to discover the means of achieving this apotheosis. As we have seen, the realization of general justice and distributive justice is intimately connected to the virtue of fortitude. Once the social order is affected by the modern democratic disease, these forms of justice wither and perish. *With them disappears the virtue of fortitude*, which kept man oriented towards his highest natural end: the realization of the common good. *Yet since people must live in society in spite of the dis-society now in place, they must also find a substitute for the virtue of fortitude.* Since politics, in its full sense, has vanished, *action* has been supplanted by *production*, and works of virtue have been replaced by the manufacture and consumption of material goods, nothing remains for man but Technology or the totality of methods necessary for an agent to transform the external world and produce something separate from himself, a house or an automobile for example.

The cardinal virtues and all the virtues that revolve around them are oriented towards the common good.

It is part of man's nature as a political animal to work for this. This is intrinsic to every man, in different degrees according to his potential; each individual, commensurate with his ability, has a share in the benefits coming from the common good. In these circumstances men are prompted to cultivate the virtue of fortitude, thus perfecting themselves *inwardly*. However, Technology, of whatever kind, is directed to a product *external* to the agent who uses it. If interiority is proper to the soul, exteriority is proper to the material world. Thus if man is no more than an economic animal, a producer and consumer of material goods, the techniques he employs to transform the material world to his benefit must themselves be material. They must create physical power greater than the power of resistance of matter. *The virtue of fortitude is replaced by this physical power*—which, by transforming the world, automatically transforms man, who is part of this world, once this power is left to itself and deprived of its subordination to the intellectual order, including the political. This is why the ancients drew a clear distinction between economics and politics, the former geared towards man's physical life, his subsistence, the latter oriented to the common good, the highest degree of which is the development of the virtuous life, without which man cannot reach the highest degree of the common good, the contemplative knowledge of God.

But once he embarks on this downward slope, man can do nothing but transform the material world and himself, perpetually, and consequently he imagines that he is continually outdoing himself in a process of unending progress; he no longer hesitates to take the place of the Creator, the first cause and end of all things. He has in his possession the means to do this: Technology in its ever more powerful forms, which harnesses the most hidden energies of nature to subjugate it, using nature as a slave at his service. *Gaudium et Spes* echoes the belief, today spread over the whole earth, that man is the culmination of the universe, and calls for the religion of man to be integrated into Catholicism. For our contemporaries, this is a "mutation" of the human species, a transition to a higher species, to the transformation of man into Superman. Once Technology is liberated from its final end, the natural and supernatural common good, it expands into a rational system of procedures, which goes from slow-paced social pressure on sectors of the social body to complete societal transformation, in order to realize what is now called the construction of a new world, a new humanity, in which man alone is master and sovereign, where he replaces the Divinity.

One may well laugh — with forced laughter! — at the distinction the ancients made between the *virtuous* good, pursued for its own sake, in harmony with practical reason oriented towards the common good; the *useful* good, sought for the sake of another good; and the *pleasurable* good, the enjoyment that follows from attaining a particular good. This *objective* classification, free of any bias, had at least the merit of placing the last two goods under the aegis of the first, as is proper when one has a modicum of common sense. But how can one elevate man to be the ultimate end of society and the world without observing that the man in question is *always* the individual, the "human person," and that good always resides in things, whether indeed real or imagined to be real? And how then can one visualize society as the mere sum of individuals, and view the world from a strictly nominalist perspective? The useful good would only be whatever satisfies the desire of the individual or the group of individuals who consciously take themselves as an end. The language of today implies this: the useful is what one avails oneself of,[35] with a reflexive verb, in which the action refers back to the subject. Utility, for the modern mind, refers to a need that can only be the private good of the one who has the need, and is emancipated from the tutelage of the common good and from the virtue of fortitude, which reinforces the common good. "The useful," Paul Janet aptly observes, reflecting the views of his times in his philosophy, "is that which is bound to our preservation and well-being."[36] *Suum utile quaerere hoc es suum esse conservare*, wrote Spinoza.[37]

But if everything becomes a matter of utility when the common good is abolished, then everything is directed towards the satisfaction of the self. Since the

[35] In French, *se servir de*, meaning "to use."
[36] *Traité élémentaire de philosophie à l'usage des classes* (1897). Janet (1823–1899) was a French philosopher known for his works on ethics. See also André Lalande, *Vocabulaire technique et critique de la philosophie*, Paris, 1951.
[37] To seek what is useful to one is to preserve one's own being. From *Ethics*, IV, 20 (1677).

human person, despite all his denials, bears within himself the imprint of the infinite Creator upon whom he depends in the depths of his being, his desires will never be able to be satisfied. He has need of more and more things to put to his use. He has need of more and more technical resources in order to fill the unbounded longing of the self for the infinite. Here we grasp, once again, the reason why technology has displaced the virtue of fortitude, to which our ancestors, willingly or unwillingly, were compelled to have recourse, as they lived in human societies perpetually exposed to the dangers of life. Mechanization is inherently linked to individualism, and to its Siamese twin, collectivism.

Marx's stroke of genius was to create a gigantic enlargement of the idolatrous Self, in which contemporary man could recognize himself. Since the commission of original sin, man has been too willing to listen to the false promise that he can achieve radical autonomy with regard to the natural common good and the universal common good, which is God: *Eritis sicut dei,* "You shall be like gods." For better or for worse (and for better rather than for worse, since man has up until now lived in society and, in spite of the expansion of the dis-society, genuine social relations persist), the virtue of fortitude has resisted the assault of the Tempter, who to attack God in His supernatural nature is constrained to attack human nature. All it took was for the satanism of Marx to *radicalize* the subversion and disruption of all enterprises undertaken by modern man, and to *subsume under the single concept of labor* all the techniques for transforming matter through which modern man seeks to manifest his transcendence and divinity: "Workers of the world, unite!"

In fact, though, man cannot avoid being a worker. "One must work in order to live," the saying goes, in order to sustain existence, which is always personal, lived in a body that individualizes it. But the popular maxim adds, with common sense, that one does not live in order to work. It is no coincidence that the word *travail*[38] originates from the Latin *tripalium*, an instrument of torture. Since the Fall, man has been compelled to earn his bread by the sweat of his brow. Marx seized upon this necessity as a lever for revolution, seeking to fashion, like a god, an entirely new world, a world geared to labor, the only world that ought to exist because it alone, he claimed, could, through dialectical necessity, engender a new and luminous world. In this world, every need would be effortlessly met; man would no longer need to work; he would be the ultimate superman.

Marxism is the logical endpoint of the prerogative granted to labor, ever since the Protestant and bourgeois rejection of the contemplative life as the highest ideal man can attain on earth through the grace of God, which, in spite of the active life some of them have led, always reaches its highest point in the saints.

In Greek and Christian tradition, society was composed of hierarchically ordered strata: the *oratores*, who held the keys to heaven and the secrets of human

[38] Work.

knowledge, philosophy, and science; the *bellatores*,[39] who through the virtue of fortitude protected states and Christendom; and the *laboratores*,[40] whose work ensured the material subsistence of society as a whole. These "classes," as we would call them today, were far from rigid. History reveals, moreover, that, from the Renaissance onward, laymen appropriated the clergy's monopoly on knowledge; during the Reformation, ecclesiastical society was dismantled; and with the [French] Revolution, these three orders were legally abolished without being replaced with other social foundations.[41]

The long struggle between the Church hierarchy and the empire played no small role in destroying the keystone of unity between these two social regimes, the civic polity and the Church, formerly allied with each other. Gradually, the foundations of this grand structure were reduced to the *laboratores*, as the other sectors declined at varying speeds. Into the ruins of secular society and the Church the destructive ferment of individualism insinuated itself, an individualism proper to an economy which has the sole purpose of serving consumers in flesh and blood, whose desires exercised such a gravitational pull on producers that guilds, those semi-natural societies, collapsed, abandoning consumers to the mercy of the producers. Man

[39] Soldiers.
[40] Workers.
[41] We can never tire of saying, with Maurras, that there was an Ancien Régime, but there is not, and never will be, a Nouveau Régime.

had no other recourse than to transform matter, and, ultimately, to transform himself, setting up his own person as the end, the only possible end, of all things.

Marx provided this corrosive concept of labor with a cohesion that industrial, commercial, and financial capitalism of the nineteenth and twentieth centuries never achieved, despite the fact that their ideologies had the same point of departure. It is in fact undeniable that liberalism has granted, and continues to grant, a privileged status to labor. This is, incidentally, the reason it is so easily permeated with socialism. However, it was only with Marx and the philosophy he injected into the industrial "society" of our times that work became the distinguishing characteristic of man, banishing both *contemplation* and *action*. Thus all human activity was reduced to *production*, in an effort to serve as the focus of the restoration of the lost unity of humanity, with work presented as the only way to achieve universal political power. Everything that *is in existence* from now on has work as its first and absolute cause, entirely subjected to its *praxis*, to its power to reshape all things.

The technology that controls work has according to Marx evolved to the point that communism is inevitable, replacing capitalism, which perfected technology. This is a *necessity*, inscribed in the very constitution of the destiny of humanity. *Why then is there still a need for the virtue of fortitude in the world? For bourgeois liberalism, it must be replaced by work. For proletarian communism, it must be eradicated and replaced with revolutionary violence, which will accelerate the march*

*of progress, of which work is the driving force. Work
will render mythical the relationship between man and
God as the cause and final end of his being, as at the
same time it suppresses all relationships of superiority
and inferiority in the new social "order."*

However, there is one condition which underscores
the degree to which Marx remains dependent on the
subjectivism and individualism proper to modern
thought: the worker can never again transfer the value
of his labor to others, as he does in the capitalist system; he no longer depends on anyone. The subversion
of values, which reduces all human activity to work
alone and grants man — ideologically! — the possibility
of being his own end exclusive of any other, implies
not only the abolition of private property and the
appropriation of the means of production by the
collectivity, as has been too hastily concluded, but
especially the reduction of man to a purely individual
entity, and the suppression of all natural — and supernatural! — social relationships. It requires violence
against those who defend these relationships through
the virtue of fortitude, and the creation of a Mon-
ster unknown to our ancestors: the communist state,
which *must* penetrate deep into the consciousness
of individuals in order to control their movements
through its governing apparatus, To achieve this, there
is only one method: individuals, whose efforts always
tend to be scattered, must be stripped of their very
selves, so that they are mystically dissolved into the
amorphous and malleable mass that their collective
self-renunciation has created.

Divinity has thus been transferred from the Self to the *Idea* of the collectivity, without the Self, athirst for the infinite, ceasing to be the Self, since this Idea is immanent in it, and coincides with it. As Simone Weil wrote, "The great beast — the collective — becomes the unique imitation of something infinitely distant from me, *and which is myself*."[42] The individual must renounce all that he has and all that he is in order to become immersed in the realm of the imaginary. For the collective exists only in thought, which adds together individual units: one plus one, plus one, etc. In reality, however, these elements are individuals separated from each other. The collective is the opium of the people, a drug that strips the human being of both intelligence and will, destroys his nature as a rational and political animal, and is administered in more or less massive doses, according to needs and circumstances, by the priests of the religion of Man. This indoctrination begins with the apparently harmless sugar-coated pill of liberal individualism. The rest follows.

Such is the "new order" being established in the world, as the permanent revolution hammers it into place and those pulling the strings of the human puppet manipulate it to their own profit. *This is the worst violence that could be committed against men in flesh and blood, with their consent, be it enthusiastic or resigned.* The society that virtually makes man disappears, and gives way to the *ergastulum*,[43] as

[42] A loose citation from *La pesenteur et la grâce* (1947).
[43] In ancient Rome a penitentiary workhouse for slaves who were shackled.

the lifeblood of communal life is replaced by immo-
bilizing shackles.

*Wherever one turns, the only response to this violence,
disguised under the purported salvific value of work,
is the virtue of fortitude in those who still possess it by
nature or by grace, and who place the common good
above their own individual good.*

IV

THE VIRTUE OF FORTITUDE OPPOSES REVOLUTIONARY VIOLENCE

S UBVERSION AND THE VIO-lence that accompanies it have not merely overthrown the hierarchy of properly human activities and completely reshaped man's mentality and social nature; prevailing everywhere, they have banished from the polity all those who still practice the virtue of fortitude. Such individuals find themselves isolated, cut off from all relations with others due to the wall of silence created around them, and, when necessary, slandered. This massive *mutation*, the massive degeneration that this word almost always implies, has penetrated the noblest and most enduring institution the world has ever known: the Catholic Church. It has done so through new "social" structures, established by laws inspired by liberal individualism.

It is undeniable that a "new Christianity" has insinuated itself within the bosom of the Church, *in sinu ac gremio Ecclesiæ* according to St. Pius X,[1]

---

[1] *Pascendi Dominici Gregis* (1907), condemning modernism.

where the contemplation of the revealed truths contained in dogma and the practice of theological virtues, which guide the faithful towards their supernatural end, have been literally sacrificed to a purely earthly *praxis*, to mere efficiency, with reliance on mere human means to save mankind. A process of secularization of the Church is underway, the outcome of which cannot be predicted. This is symbolized by the cassock thrown aside, a radical *aggiornamento*, an "irreversible" adaptation to the "inalienable" demands of the modern world, which is consumed by the fever of democracy, whether liberal or collectivist. The Church of the "new priests" is now centered on man, on the secularized human person who takes himself as his own end, on his desires, aspirations, claims, and demands.

Man is no longer measured by his definition, that of a political animal ordered towards the common good, to which he must submit. No longer strengthened for this purpose by the virtue of fortitude, he becomes the measure, the only measure, of all things *and of God Himself*, now obligated to adapt Himself to modern man's mentality and to his subjectivity, held to be inviolable and sacred.

A complete reversal of the supernatural order is taking place before our eyes: theology seeks to be anthropocentric, without fearing any contradiction; the transcendence of God yields to the multiform imperatives of immanence; catechesis is no longer subject to doctrine, but to the stipulations of an autonomous conscience, the drives of the unconscious, the sexual instinct, and the thousand and one ravings of the dis-society; the liturgy obeys all the whims of the ringmaster and entertainment producer; authority turns into opportunism and timidly yields to public opinion created and managed by pressure groups or the bureaucracy it is entrenched in, following the example of the *pays légal*[2]; the supernatural becomes natural; its transcendent order, of which the Church was formerly the guardian, is emptied of its content, to the benefit of a method for the redemption of humanity copied from the machinations of the permanent revolution; in turn, great numbers of the clergy aspire to build the kingdom of God on earth through mere human words, or the Word of God redirected from its meaning; faith becomes political ideology; those who are near us are replaced by those who are distant; the *man of God* gives up his "magical" power and changes into a *man like any other*, a modern man, who, as such, does not see anything as being beyond him and gives free rein to his thirst for power instead of cultivating the virtue of fortitude and resisting the assaults made against the flesh.

Subversion is firmly entrenched within the Church, exploiting its influence to destroy it from within, to do violence to souls and to establish, with a hypocrisy which is not always unconscious, especially in the hierarchy, a form of *clerical Caesarism* which penetrates to the very core of the human being and substitutes

---

[2] The legal country, referring to the state bureaucracy and political parties, as opposed to the real country (*pays réel*), society and, in a broader sense, the nation. Maurras popularized this distinction.

itself for the will of God, clearly stated in Scripture: *Hæc est enim voluntas Dei, sanctificatio vestra.*[3]

This new Christianity, stripped of its supernatural essence, has been inflated to the point of rupture by a "social Christianity," which is nothing more than a copy, overlaid with a vague, barely deistic religiosity, of one of the many varieties of leftism, liberalism, and communism. The collusion between the new Christianity and leftist currents of thought was inevitable. We are now in the presence of the very mystery of our time: it enables us to understand why the cardinal virtue of fortitude, highly esteemed over centuries through divine grace and Catholic tradition, has now been banished from the modern mentality, including among Christians, and why the mystique of violence has taken its place. One need only read the works of contemporary theologians and the pastoral letters of bishops, as well as the constitutions of Vatican II, to see that fortitude plays no role in them. If by chance it is mentioned, it is only to be reviled, vilified, and condemned as the ultimate sin, which cannot be forgiven. This is in reality not a case of collusion between two disparate currents of thought: they are different, but have the same source. This was already foreseen by Count de Saint-Simon, in his apologia for industrialism and his vision of a "new regime" for humanity, which he advocated.[4]

---

[3] For this is the will of God, your sanctification (1 Thes. 4:3).
[4] Henri de Saint-Simon (French political and economic theorist, 1760–1825), in all his work and especially in a book with this remarkable title, *Le Nouveau Christianisme*, 1825.

Too little attention has been paid to the fact that "industrial society," the great innovation of our time, which has displaced most of the natural forms in previous societies, was born in the Christian West, and *nowhere else*. Even less remarked upon is that this is the result of the Catholic Church's slow decline, following its remarkable resurgence after the Council of Trent. It was during the Enlightenment that de-Christianization, which had already been promoted behind the scenes, launched its direct assault on Europe, hardly meeting with any resistance on the part of the clergy, who had succumbed to the process of the secularization of Christianity. Notably, both secular and ecclesiastical society were simultaneously attacked, in their critical activities and their very structures. The former found its ultimate purpose under assault for being an obstacle to individual liberty: the common good, once safeguarded by monarchs and the nobility, the *bellatores* of the Middle Ages, was now seen by the *intelligentsia* as a weapon of despots used against the human person already freed from the stranglehold of the Church through the triumph of Protestantism in the minds of the people. The society of the Church was headed by a succession of mediocre popes, preoccupied with political disputes, and Benedict XIV. This pontiff, who reigned for eighteen years, adopted an extremely conciliatory stance when confronted with the demands of Catholic and Protestant rulers and the mentality of the *philosophes*. The hierarchy no longer gave the impression of being at the head of the only supernatural society

of persons that could exist, the result of the elimination of their essential incommunicability through the
divine imprint conferred by means of the sacrament
of baptism and adherence to the same faith. The
result was that within what remained of Catholic
Christianity there was a general weakening of the
sense of the supernatural, which freed men from the
bonds that united them within the Church, inclining
them, depending on their temperament, to religious
individualism, where the only remaining unifying
factor would be natural religion, the seat of a distant,
unknown, unknowable God with no connection to
human society. With grace no longer strengthening
nature, man's political nature and his subordination
to the common good then have even less meaning.

What, then, remains to unite men, if not technology, work, the economy, and the foundation of a
new type of "society" with an individualist orientation which, as such, can have no other end than the
material happiness of one and all? The promoters
of the *Encyclop*édie,[5] whose influence among the
ruling classes and the clergy was enormous, perceived
this clearly. Only an industrial society, ordered to the
individual consumer in flesh and blood, could be the
heir to both the Ancien Régime and the Catholic
Church, both of which were outdated in their eyes.

This jettisoning of the common good to the profit
of private interests then inevitably goes back from the

[5] General encyclopedia published in France between 1751 and
1772, the work of the *philosophes*, who intended it to further the
thought of the Enlightenment.

end of the process to the beginning, in other words, to the producers, who are all consumers as well, with an unavoidable outcome: the struggle among different levels of producers for a share of the profit. When the *Encyclopédie, ou Dictionnaire raisonné des sciences, des arts et des métiers,*[6] compiled by a cadre of men of letters, claimed to offer its public the general principles of technical methods, "which give rise to arts so useful to life, which are perfected every day," as John Locke had already stated in *An Essay Concerning Human Understanding,*[7] it was merely continuing the direction given to modern philosophy by Descartes: to make it strictly independent of religion and politics, contrary to the earlier Aristotelian scholasticism; to destroy the solidarity between *contemplation, action,* and *production*; to eliminate the first two of these, to the sole advantage of the third, which, according to the predication in Descartes' *Discours de la Méthode,* would make man "the master of nature," elevating the hard-working *Ego* to the summit of the universe.

The unrestrained apologia for the technical arts, which reverberates throughout the Encyclopédie, and the establishment of the new industrial society proposed by its contributors, work together in the ruthless war against the Catholic Church, in order to replace the only society of persons that could exist with an association of all men taken as individuals, each pursuing the only form of happiness still

---

[6] The complete name of the *Encyclopédie, The Encyclopédie, or Systematic Dictionary of the Sciences, Arts, and Trades.*
[7] 1689.

possible under the reign of a universal Technology:
the individual, material good of each human being.
General justice no longer exists, and consequently
neither does the virtue of fortitude which defends it.
Distributive justice is reduced to nothing more than
the allocation, by the new "society" now established,
of material and financial benefits to those who work
towards its prosperity. The roles of the *oratores* and
bellatores have come to an end: the Europe which
replaces Christendom, now vanished, leaves room
only for the *laboratores*, represented in this age by
the bourgeoisie. What need is there now for moral
and political fortitude, when man is in the process
of domesticating all the energies of nature for his
own benefit?

Modern industrial "society," whose vision, set forth
by the Enlightenment, was founded on the liberation
of the human person from whatever is not his own
personal good, with the consequent defense of his
inalienable rights, is only the latest metamorphosis of
Christianity, which bursts into individualism as soon
as the ecclesial institution established by Christ for
the supernatural salvation of its members begins to
totter and develop fissures. Under the designation of a
"society of abundance," towards which capitalism leads,
or the "perfect society," in which the forms of alien-
ation to which the human person is subject will be
completely removed, this industrial "society" — which
claims to be the only possible society of our time, as
evidenced by the current absorption of politics into
purely economic concerns — is the product of the

collapse of the vertical dimension of Redemption into the horizontal.

Through the power of technology, man will soon be freed from all evils. The ideology of Progress, which permeates this technological paradigm, convinces modern man that he can now be certain of attaining happiness here below. This then is how the vast majority of our contemporaries conceive of their existence: "Eat and drink, for tomorrow we die." Should a crisis arise in this march forward towards happiness, it will sooner or later be overcome by the further development of man's technical skills, which have rendered the exercise of the virtue of fortitude unnecessary. Moreover, there are always culprits to blame for any crisis: they are the "reactionaries," the idolaters of the past, despite the fact that a clean slate has been made of that past. It will suffice to eliminate them through revolutionary violence, and Progress will once again resume its course towards its only possible goal: the material salvation of individuals throughout the whole world, transcending their individual characteristics, be they racial, national, social, or even familial, and replacing the pitiful supernatural salvation that the Church promises to its faithful.

If we call revolution the complete overthrow of an order, then it is clear that this "*New Christianity*," as Count de Saint-Simon dares to call it, which consists of reorienting individual salvation from heaven to earth, is indeed a revolution. Moreover, if every revolution first takes hold in minds before being translated into laws and conduct, then it is equally evident that *this new Christianity itself is the Revolution par excellence*. More than that: *it coincides in time with the Permanent Revolution* raging in the world for the past two or three centuries. In other words, the new Christianity, which seeks to establish an industrial society (the foundations of which had been laid in the Enlightenment) as the savior of the human person in place of the Catholic Church, and the Revolution that followed, gradually winning over all the countries of the world, are one and the same Christian heresy. This is the gravest and most universal heresy there could be, one that has ushered in the most ruthless of all wars of religion: the war between faith in God and faith in Man. This war exerts on civil society (composed not of aggregated individuals, but of smaller communities, of which the family is the ultimate component), and on the Church, which it is completely secularizing, the most inhuman forms of violence: it seeks to annihilate in man, if it were possible, both nature and grace.

If we hold *firmly*, through the virtue of fortitude and the gift of fortitude that strengthens it, to the obvious fact that the Gospel, WITHOUT the Church (the guardian of faith and morals), WITHOUT Tradition (which preserves them intact), WITHOUT the metaphysics of the human mind (which the Greeks transmitted to all men of all times and places), and WITHOUT the complementary certainty that man is a political animal subject to the common good of the various societies into which he is integrated, *can have no other interpreter than individual reason, left to all the passions that the virtue of fortitude no longer restrains and to the most terrible of these, the passion "to be like gods,"* through changing the focus of salvation from heaven to earth. THEN, and only THEN, will we understand that this same Gospel can *be changed* into an agent of corruption of incalculable reach, degenerating into a religion of Man, with the overturning of the entire order of values that this new religion brings in its wake.

Without the Church, without Tradition, without the philosophy of common sense, without the primacy of the political common good, the Gospel is changed into a revolutionary agent, denying all supernatural and natural realities because it makes of the human person an entity with limitless rights, and the principle and end of all things.[8] Man appropriates to himself the attributes of God. Jesus becomes merely the model of the human conscience, the measure of the universe. The priest who imitates Him places himself above ecclesiastical law, above civil law, and even above morality itself, and considers himself invested, through an appalling obligation of conscience, with the power to destroy a world that resists the demands of divinized Man and to rebuild another out of nothing, one that

---

[8] This is what the *Nouvelle Droite*, made up of anti-Christian intellectuals, is incapable of understanding: it blames Christianity for all evils, while the source of these evils is an inverted Christianity. This is why the *Nouvelle Droite* shares many ideas of the left and *cannot not share them*. [The New Right in France opposes liberal democracy and capitalism and promotes a form of democracy freed from oligarchy. It is influenced by a humanistic form of Marxism.]

conforms to his commitments. How can this superhuman task be accomplished without civil and religious war, without resorting to violence, unchecked by any divine or human law, a task for which the "theology of Revolution" has been made the apologia? There is no longer any human or divine common good to which the unrestrained human person is subordinated. There is no longer a society: it implodes. The Church has entered the stage of "self-demolition."

Far from merely following subversion up to its most intense phases in order not to "lose touch" with the people, the revolutionary Gospel precedes it, and *is the cause of it*, the sole origin of it, for it bears within itself something more than yeast gone bad: the divinization of the Self. Among all the religions of the world, Christianity alone teaches that God became Man so that man might become God, but with the proviso that man give up his Self, and renounce the appropriation of his *person* to himself— "You are not your own," says the Apostle [1 Cor. 6:19] — however without renouncing his *essence* as a rational, political animal created by God: "Thy will be done, and not mine." This is where the Gospel, as the Catholic Church has received it from Our Lord Jesus Christ to be announced to mankind without alteration, confronts the revolutionary Gospel.

For since the proclamation of the Gospel, the Self has only one possible disguise left: the mask of purporting to be God, the parody of divine knowledge and divine love, spectacularly displayed on the stage of this world. Before God, man can only become God through participation in the divine life by *dispossessing himself of himself,* or mimicking Him by *appropriating Him to himself.* There are a thousand ways to use God to serve oneself, but all these metamorphoses come down to *aping Him.* After Christianity, man is left with just ARTIFICE, with TECHNIQUES through which he recreates the world, reconstructs society, fashions the "new man," effectuates a new "redemption," "liberates" and "saves" man. All current deviations, errors, and attempts to subvert the human and divine order are Christian heresies. Today, the world is the victim of the madness of these errors, because a good many Christians, deprived of the virtue of fortitude, no longer impose the straitjacket they deserve on the falsifiers of the Gospel. This is because these Christians increasingly do not *resist* the universal aberration and refuse to *attack* it with the weapons of nature and grace.

Marxist revolutionary violence, liberal weakness and tolerance, and so-called "evangelical" violence all have the same origin: the rejection of God and the divinization of individual and collective Man, or more precisely the use of the idea of God, emptied of all its natural and supernatural content, and filled with the demands of the Self, which are destructive of all traditional societies.

We then comprehend that we have to change our thinking when we analyze the essence and reach of the virtue of fortitude. The virtue of fortitude has as its end not only resistance to murderers of the common good, especially in "hot wars," but also unwavering resolve in the face of protean dangers that break up what remains of society and the Church, in other words, before the threats to *the natural and supernatural ends of the human spirit in the throes of the "cold war."* While creating breaches in contemporary civil and ecclesiastical *dis-society*, revolutionary violence, facilitated by individualistic liberalism and the so-called rights of the human person — now severed from his traditional social communities and, for the Christian, from his allegiance to the Mystical Body of Christ — has only one goal: to take control of the State, the Method of methods, the Power above all other powers, in order to establish its dominion over the poor human beings in its thrall. It must eradicate in them, as their source, the natural and supernatural common good, and the practice of the virtue of fortitude and even its existence. The intellectually and morally corrupted priest is one with the representative of the government, who reciprocally sees himself in the priest. For one as well as for the other, who have both denied the transcendent realities of secular life and the Sacred, *all means are good* and the greatest of all means is *the modern State*. The day they jointly take hold of the State, it will be the end.

This is the end towards which revolutionary violence is striving, *if we do not first oppose it with the virtue of fortitude*, which we still possess by a kind of miracle, with all it requires and all the acts that flow from it, involving both resistance AND attack.

V

THE VIRTUES ASSOCIATED
WITH FORTITUDE

HE STATE OF DIS-SOCIETY, where natural communities, the nation itself, as well as the Catholic Church, fractured into a thousand different chapels according to the thousand catechisms, the thousand liturgies, and the thousand versions of Sacred Scripture which have been adopted and tolerated since Vatican II, calls for not only a reassessment of the purpose of the virtue of fortitude but also of the virtues related to it, which are an extension of it.

The first among these is *magnanimity*, a virtue which derives its name from what is truly great, just as fortitude derives its name from what is truly difficult.[1] According to Aristotle, St. Thomas, and common sense, the magnanimous man is one whose soul strives to act with greatness, that is, "through the best use of the greatest thing" (*in optimo usa rei maximae*).[2]

---

[1] The word "fortitude" and the French equivalent, *force*, are both derived from the Latin *fortis*, meaning "strong."

[2] *ST*, II-II, q. 129, art. 1, c.

"Now, the things[3] that man makes use of are external to himself. Among these, the highest place belongs to *honor*, which is closest to virtue, since it is an effective testimony (*testificatio existens*) given to it, since it is also offered to God and to the most perfect individuals, and since, finally, men despise all else in order to acquire honor and avoid shame."[4] To be thus elevated to the level of what is highest, honor, implies greatness of soul in the subject.[5]

Magnanimity is a specific virtue, which, like every virtue, entails the rejection of both excess and deficiency. The magnanimous man aims at what is greatest (*ad maxima tendit*). What is greatest is the service of the common good of the state and of the universal common good, which is God. This *objective* function, ordered to a transcendent reality, has an effect on the subject when he carries it out in accord with practical reason, which directs him to accomplish this as he ought, that is to say, by keeping to the happy medium, with a proper estimation of himself, and by aiming for only for that of which he is worthy in light of the end he pursues and attains. As always, in a philosophy of common sense, it is the end that dictates the means and their use and that determines the subject's attitude it; if that end is great, it demands from the subject greatness of soul.

Here, we rediscover general justice — long ignored by modern egalitarianism and subjectivism — which is directed to the common good in its two forms,

---

[3] *Res* in Latin.
[4] Ibid, in a loose citation.
[5] *ST*, II-II, q. 129, art. 2, c.

human and divine, and extends into distributive justice, according to whether the effort to realize it is greater or lesser. Thus, distributive justice confers greater or lesser honor to those who have shown more or less magnanimity in their actions aimed at the common good: the hero is honored by the state for his greatness of soul, and the saint by the Church for the same reason. Honor is the subjective side, the other dimension of the objective end pursued, the counterpart of the virtue of fortitude. Among the twenty or so meanings that Littré[6] attributes to the word *honor* and terms related to or derived from it, two stand out that appear to be essential: the first is the objective meaning, "The great regard accorded to the virtue, *to courage*, and to accomplishments," as in the expression "to do honor to one's birth" or "to do honor to the truth," which refer to realities which do not depend on us. The second is the subjective meaning, which is "the sentiment that makes one desire to preserve self-esteem and the esteem of others." The following verses from Boileau[7] perfectly illustrate this subordination of the subject to the object:

> The only sound honor
> Is always to take truth as a guide.

Honor is the reward granted by society to the individual who practices the virtue of magnanimity. The

---

[6] Émile Littré (1801–1881), French lexicographer, best known for his great *Dictionnaire de la langue française*, 1863–1973.

[7] Nicolas Boileau (1636–1711), French poet and critic. The verses are from *Satire XI*, "Sur l'honneur." The *Satires* (1657–1705) were aimed at contemporary Parisian life.

magnanimous man seeks this specific good, honor,[8] which derives precisely from the exercise of the virtue of fortitude. "By virtue of his lofty intentions, he must accomplish that which elevates and flee that which diminishes. It is greatness to be benevolent, to give of one's self (*quod sit communicativus*), and to return more than one has received (*plurium retributivus*). The magnanimous man willingly undertakes these acts of virtue, not for their own sake, but because they have the character of excellence."[9]

Now what greater act is there than to give one's life for one's country in war or for God in martyrdom? Magnanimity is thus a part of fortitude, whose intimate relation to the common good we have already seen. "It is subordinated to fortitude as a secondary virtue is to a principal virtue."[10] If greatness of soul can enhance all the virtues, and make them greater,[11] it especially crowns the virtue of fortitude when evidenced in attacks. Magnanimity is distinguished from fortitude in its firmness in pursuit of good, while fortitude, as we have seen, is firmness in resistance to

---

[8] *ST*, II-II, q. 129, art. 4, c. and ad 1.

[9] Ibid. ad. 2. De Corte notes: For the record, we reference the only book in French dedicated to the subject, extremely scholarly, by Father R. A. Gauthier, OP, *La Magnanimité, L'idéal de la grandeur dans la philosophie païenne et dans la théologie chrétienne*, Paris, 1951. This work is flawed by a philosophy inspired by subjectivism, to which Dominican scholars have succumbed for years, whose thesis in our estimation is false from beginning to end. For a demonstration of this see our study *L'Éthique à Nicomaque, Introduction à la Politique*, in *Mélanges offerts à Joseph Moreau*, Paris, 1978.

[10] *ST*, II-II, q. 129, art. 5, c.

[11] Ibid, art. 4, ad 3.

evil. The self-confidence that every magnanimous man has instills in him the hope that he will be victorious in the great enterprises he undertakes, and this is the second way to attain the virtue of fortitude.[12]

The adaptation of the virtue of magnanimity to the situation today is parallel to what we have said regarding fortitude. It is no longer merely a question of facing the danger of death in combat or martyrdom, but of personally resisting the mortal dangers that now assault society and the Church, guardian of the faith. Similarly, greatness of soul is no longer evident only in the conquest of honor, esteem, renown, glory, or the approval of a great number of persons (*in multorum notitiam et approbationem*),[13] because one has a high position in society which corresponds to the requirements of distributive justice, which themselves satisfy general justice, through their activities undertaken in view of the natural and supernatural common good. Instead, magnanimity today demands the renunciation of the desire to obtain and preserve the esteem of others and self-esteem. It calls for striving to accomplish great things with humility and a spirit of littleness, yet with firmness and steadfastness, wherever the circumstances of birth and vocation have placed us.

Greatness of soul and humility are not at all incompatible.[14] In the civil and ecclesiastical dis-society in which we are immersed, greatness of soul is found in the humble tasks of daily life, according to practical

[12] Ibid., art. 6, c and ad 1 and 2. See also art. 7.
[13] *ST*, II-II, q. 132, art. 1, c.
[14] Ibid., q. 129, ad 4.

reason and the teaching of Our Lord Jesus Christ,[15] in order to restore, little by little, even if the task seems never-ending, society, the setting of the common good, and the Church, the conduit of faith, hope, and charity. Society and the Church were not rebuilt otherwise after the fall of the Roman Empire. The first society gradually took shape around the *pater familias* and his labor, and became the common good of a few who were dedicated to maintaining it because their very survival demanded it. The Christendom of the Middle Ages was built around monasteries, little centers of supernatural light and peace, scattered across the immense territory of a fragmented Europe. Christendom, with these humble beginnings, was built up stone by stone until crosses triumphed at the tops of cathedrals.

To accomplish little things while aiming for great things: to restore society and the Church, even and perhaps especially knowing that one will be laboring during the night, never seeing the dawn here below; to transmit this heritage to one's children, to one's circle of family and friends, necessarily restricted in a time such as ours; to renounce *honors* — in the plural, as Péguy[16] wrote — in order to uphold the honor of man and the honor of God; to hope against all hope, *contra spem in spe*, with the joy and fortitude of the Apostle, without expecting any reward from others,

[15] See the words of St. Teresa of Avila to her nuns on this subject: "Everything which separates you from reason" — *from its ability to find its end in reality* — "separates you from God."

[16] Charles Péguy (1873–1914), French poet and essayist, fallen in battle during World War I.

this is the magnanimity required today. Perhaps this magnanimity is greater than the one Aristotle and St. Thomas observed among the great men of their own times. It is a question of nothing less than rekindling the flame of the eternal amid the elusive shadows which carry us off towards tomorrows of disillusionment. It is a matter of nothing less than preserving and transmitting the gifts that the Creator of the political animal and the Savior of sinful man constantly bestow on us.

Indeed every era has its own form of greatness of soul. The hero of past centuries has given way to the fathers and mothers of families, these great adventurers of the modern world, as we again recall the words of Péguy,[17] tirelessly striving to pass on to their children the heritage of eternity. The harsh mortifications of the Desert Fathers and the faithfulness in little things practiced by St. Thérèse of the Child Jesus testify to the same greatness of soul, which is open to the Infinite. The following assertion of the "little saint of Lisieux" is imbued with this form of magnanimity, new yet essentially the same throughout all of history: "It is not necessary to perform spectacular deeds, but rather to hide from the eyes of others and from oneself."[18] The "transformation" of man, the Little Way teaches us, does not consist of transforming the world and oneself through the power of material means, but in the elevation of weakness to the level of strength through the humble means of everyday life, *in taking up one's*

[17] See his article "L'Argent" in *Cahiers de la Quinzaine* (1913) for Péguy's thoughts on honor in the home and workplace.
[18] *Histoire d'une âme*, 1898. (*The Story of a Soul.*)

tasks and going from the most basic finite realities to
the infinite.

This is the school of magnanimity: never to
renounce the earthly and heavenly goals of man.
"*Where would your merit be,*" St. Thérèse teaches
us, and confirms by her example,"*if you only had to
fight when you felt courageous? What does it matter
if you feel no courage as long as you act as though you
did!*"[19] Could there be in the world a form of greatness of soul more apt to invite all people to practice
this virtue? This magnanimity is accessible even to
those whom the modern dis-society counts as nothing
because they go against the tide. The Gospel proclaims
it in the secular as well as the sacred domain: *Qui
fidelis est in minimo et in majori fidelis est.*[20]

The teaching of St. Thérèse here seems to us to be
inexhaustible. In his homily at the Mass for her can-
onization, Pius XI had already stressed, "*If this way of
spiritual childhood became widespread, how easily the
reformation of human society could be achieved, which
we proposed at the beginning of our pontificate.*"[21]
In the judgment of Aristotle, later reiterated by St.
Thomas and true for his time: "The magnanimous

[19] From the memoirs of Sister Marie of the Trinity, one of the
novices under St. Thérèse's care, only excerpts of which have been
published. This quotation appeared in print for the first time in
the 1907 edition of *Histoire d'une âme*, in a section devoted to
the Carmelite sisters' memories of Thérèse.
[20] Luke 16:10, He that is faithful in that which is least, is faithful
also in that which is greater. See also Luke 19:17.
[21] For a development of this theme, see our *Essai sur la fin d'une
civilisation*, Paris, 1949. The English translation, *On the Death of
a Civilization*, was published by Arouca Press in 2023.

man is not *microkindynos*, brave only in small things, but *megalokindynos*, brave in great things."²² Today, both ends of the spectrum must be joined, beginning, as one must, with the first. If it is true that "excellence is the greatest human desire, and glory, which is closely linked to it, is highly desirable"²³ to the ancient type of the magnanimous man, the magnanimous man who lives at a time when the hierarchy of ends and the hierarchy of men are reversed must renounce this desire, not out of contempt or indifference, but simply because what only matters is the esteem *of a happy few*,²⁴ of a few who, like him, strive to return to the essential and understand that all great things began as small things.

Thus the greatest danger today for those who strive to practice magnanimity is no longer found in the vices of an excess of greatness of soul that St. Thomas analyzes, such as presumption, ambition, or vainglory,²⁵ but in pusillanimity, as in the fearful servant of the parable, who digs a hole in the earth where he buries the money he has received instead of trying to make it bear fruit, and is therefore punished by his master.²⁶ This small-mindedness is especially prevalent among those who lose sight of the purpose of small

²² *ST*, II-II, q. 129, art. 5, ad 2. Aquinas uses the Greek terms taken from Aristotle.
²³ Ibid. q. 132, art. 4, c.
²⁴ Italicized words are in English in the original, a reference to Shakespeare's *Henry V* and the king's rallying speech to his soldiers before battle.
²⁵ *ST*, II-II, q. 130 to 132.
²⁶ Ibid, q. 133, art. 1, c, referring to Matthew 25 and Luke 19.

things and by the same token fail to recognize the importance of the details that make up the whole, of the parts that constitute the whole.

One example of this is the abandonment of clerical dress. St. Thomas tells us that disregard for one's own condition, and for the outward signs that express it, leads to the renunciation of the great things one was originally capable of achieving.[27] This applies to a father of a family, who, for fear of what people will say, tolerates his daughters' negligence in dress or the slovenly appearance of his sons. In both cases, the excuse is always the same: these are trivial matters! There is an apathy in the pusillanimous man, a complacence that reveals his individualistic liberalism, and, at the same time, his weakness.

The second complementary virtue of fortitude is *magnificence*,[28] which, like magnanimity, must also be adapted to our modern era. "The function of the magnificent man is to do great things. But everything that regards what is personal is small in comparison to divine worship or community affairs," St. Thomas writes. "Thus, the magnificent man does not primarily seek to be lavish towards himself, not that he does not seek his own good, but simply because to do so is not something great."[29] This virtue has to do with the perfection of works of art, namely, that they should

[27] Ibid. and ad 2.
[28] As noted below, this virtue involves undertaking great things and persevering under trial. It includes donation of money for communal needs.
[29] *ST*, II-II, q. 134, art. 1, ad 3.

be great in quantity, richness, or dignity.[30] Its end is the greatness of a work of art, especially one that gives honor to God. Its primary effect is to order souls towards sanctity and religion.[31] In its object, magnificence, like fortitude, aspires to something transcendent and difficult, as it makes great demands. The vice opposed to magnificence is obviously miserliness.

The modern adaptation of magnificence is analogous to that of magnanimity. It is clear that the financial means of most people today who remain anchored to the common good of society and the Church do not equal those of Lorenzo the Magnificent,[32] the Renaissance popes, or Louis XIV! Yet, even with their income, however reduced it may be by modern taxation which tends to equalize wealth, they can still use their resources to purchase relatively inexpensive things, which can elicit a real, lasting aesthetic reaction, rather than spending on horrible utilitarian trinkets or on trendy products that are out of date as soon as they are produced. In this way, the love of beauty can still be maintained in small but lively social circles, where magnificence on a small scale still has an impact, particularly within the home.

Whereas in the times of Aristotle and St. Thomas, the miserly man is one who always undertakes a small project that does not cost too much, or else one who, after incurring great expense, is deprived the grandeur

---

[30] Ibid., art. 2, c.
[31] Ibid, ad 2 and 3.
[32] Lorenzo de' Medici (1449–1492), Florentine statesman and munificent patron of the arts

and beauty of things through his smallness of spirit,[33] today's magnificent man will purchase a beautiful piece of furniture, a fine engraving, or a beautiful rug, as well as little things, in order to maintain at least the hope that great and beautiful things will be loved.

In this regard, it must be admitted that in most cases clergymen today do not overindulge the faithful with their churches, which they have stripped of their humble riches under the pretext of "evangelical poverty," to the great benefit of antique dealers and traders in second-hand goods! They take small-mindedness to its extreme! It is thus fitting to reserve our modest munificent gifts for those priests and the very few bishops who have preserved deep concern for the truth of the faith and the splendor of the liturgy.

Among the four virtues that revolve around fortitude, much like planets around their sun, *patience* remains unchanged, as well as perseverance. "It is the role of patience," says St. Augustine, "to enable us to endure evils without faltering and to prevent us from abandoning, through weakness, the goods that lead us to greater things."[34] Yet, its action becomes more intense at a time when the dis-society has put down permanent roots and the self-destruction of the Church is still far from being contained or suppressed.

While patience is not the highest of virtues, since "the virtues that constitute the good incline a man more directly to the good than those which impede

---

[33] I.e., since he was reluctant to make the expenditure. *ST*, II-II, q. 135, art. 1, c.
[34] Ibid., q. 136, art. 1, c.

what leads him away from the good,"[35] it holds a place of utmost importance in the attitude one must have towards the evils which are the greatest of all since they strike at the very heart of the natural and supernatural common good and deeply wound the political animal created by God and the children of Adam redeemed by Christ. Thus the virtue of patience cannot be exercised, according to St. Thomas, without the help of grace, for "the good for the sake of which one is willing to endure evils" and the sorrow they bring "is willed and loved more than the good the deprivation of which causes the suffering that we bear patiently."[36]

How can one endure the catastrophe which both society and the Church are enthusiastically hastening towards without the highest of goods, that of grace? If it is enough for a few willing people, armed with the proper means, to set themselves to restoring the common good, this will also require gratuitous aid from God,[37] and if the restoration is delayed, still more patience will be needed and more divine assistance.

It is interesting that St. Thomas does not set forth a list of vices opposed to patience, as he does with other virtues. We now understand the reason for this: the exercise of patience must be without limits, or, more precisely, as St. Thomas asserts, following St. John Chrysostom, without any other limit than the extent of the wrongs done to God. *In this case, patience must rise up against those who commit evil (insiliat in*

[35] Ibid., q. 136, art. 2, c.
[36] Ibid., art. 3, c.
[37] Ibid, ad 2.

eum qui mala facit).[38] "To overlook offenses against God is most wicked," says St. Thomas (*injurias Dei dissimulare nimis est impium*).[39] This also holds for the public good, according to St. Augustine: "the precepts of patience are not opposed to the good of the republic, since in order to preserve that good we fight against our enemies."[40]

As for *perseverance*, it is "a specific virtue that involves persisting for as long as necessary, in the practice of the preceding virtues and of all the others."[41] It is a virtue that grafts itself onto fortitude, since its purpose is to overcome the daunting character of the evils that increase as they endure.[42] For this reason, perseverance must last for all of human life: it belongs to its nature to persist to the very end (*usque ad finem*). One must fight for faith, hope, and charity, which have as their object the ultimate purpose of all of life, and which today are more under attack than ever before. One must combat the enemies of true society, and its caricatures, the "permissive society" and the "totalitarian society." And this without failing, *usque ad finem certaminis*, until the end of the battle,[43] even if this can only be dimly perceived. Must we add that perseverance, because the human will is by nature changeable (*cum liberum arbitrium de se sit vertibile*), requires the help

[38] Ibid., art. 4, ad 3.
[39] Ibid., q. 188, art. 3, ad 1.
[40] Ibid., q. 136, art. 4, ad 3.
[41] Ibid., q. 137, art. 1, c.
[42] Ibid., art. 2, c.
[43] Ibid., art. 1, ad 2.

of God, which is never refused to those who beg for it to achieve an end in conformity with natural and supernatural justice?[44]

It is in this way that man will be able to fight against the vices that are opposed to perseverance, against indolence, which abandons the common good of society and the Church by giving in to sadness brought on when one is deprived of pleasure or when one gives oneself over to just the enjoyment of lesser goods; and against stubbornness in holding to subjective opinions for and against everything, with no concern for the flexibility required in determining means of action nor for the firmness demanded by the pursuit of their objective end.[45]

The catastrophes that today disrupt society and the Church have no other origin than the "love of novelties" (*praesumptio novitatum*), which essentially harnesses these opinions. To display their superiority (*manifestatio propriae excellentiae*), those who occupy positions of power in contemporary "society" and the Church obstinately seek after novelty because it generally evokes the admiration of others (*novitates quas homines solent admirari*) and keeps them at the forefront of what is current.[46] The persevering man,

---

[44] Ibid., art. 4, c.

[45] Ibid., q. 138, art. 1 and 2.

[46] Ibid., q. 132, art. 5, c. See the words of Paul VI at his general audience, July 2, 1969: "We want to make ours the great words of the council, *the words that define its spirit*, and which, in a dynamic synthesis, *form the minds of all those who refer to it*, whether or not they are in the Church. The word 'novelty,' simple, in wide use, very agreeable to men of today, is one of those words. *This*

on the other hand, does not have this concern about openness to the world and its praises: like the Apostle, he strives to "redeem the time" (*redimere tempus*), and through an act of the will continually renewed, to be open to what is eternal in heaven and on earth, for "the days are evil" (*dies mali sunt*) [Eph. 5:16].

It is important to observe that St. Thomas concludes his treatise *De Fortitudine*[47] with two questions, the first dedicated to the gift of fortitude, and the second to the Decalogue. Both deal with divine justice, both natural and supernatural, as we have shown above. It is beyond human strength to bring every good work to completion and to avoid every threatening danger (*quod quidem excedit naturam humanam*). It is the work of the Holy Spirit to sustain man in this task "that He may bring him to eternal life, which is the end of all good works and the deliverance from all dangers. The Holy Spirit infuses into the soul a certain confidence in this result and expels the contrary fear."[48]

Today when there abound a kind of charismatic delirium and an extravagant gift of tongues, against which St. Paul had already protested — (*sobria sit ebrietas Spiritus!*[49]) — it is urgent to recall the fourth beatitude which corresponds to the gift of fortitude: "Blessed are those who hunger and thirst for justice, for they shall be satisfied" [Matt. 5:6]. The justice spoken

word has been given to us as an order, as a program." The original Italian of Paul's address is *novità*, which has been translated as "novelty" in English, but could also be rendered "innovation."

[47] Referring to the relevant questions in the *ST*: II-II, q. 123-140.

[48] *ST*, II-II, q. 139, art. 1, c.

[49] May the inebriation of the Spirit be sober, see Eph. 5:18.

of here is not the demand for the perishable goods of this world, with which modern man is obsessed, but for the loving action of God for the sake of salvation in Our Lord Jesus Christ, which man receives and by which he is justified. He is called *just* who abandons himself to what is willed by the general justice of God and to whom God renders distributive justice according to his works. The God of revelation is now, through the incarnation of His Son, the universal common Good that surpasses all knowledge and is the transcendent end of all properly Christian activity.

"The connection between justice and fortitude consists in this, that fortitude has for its object difficult undertakings. Now it is very difficult not only to carry out virtuous deeds that are commonly called works of justice (*opera justitiae*)," aimed at the supernatural common Good as revealed, "but even more to perform them with that insatiable desire that can be described as the hunger and thirst for justice."[50] St. Thomas then clarifies further: "One can understand here not only particular justice, but also general justice, which extends to all acts of virtue, in which whatever is hard is the object of the gift of fortitude."[51]

If this is the case with regard to the relationship between the virtue of fortitude and fortitude which is the gift of the Holy Spirit, the same must be said of its connection to the commandments of God as formulated in the Decalogue. Indeed, the divine law

---

[50] *ST*, II-II, q. 139, art. 2, c.
[51] Ibid., ad 1.

has as its end the union of man with God, the supernatural common good of all those whom He saves
through the gift of fortitude, whereas human laws are
ordered towards the temporal common good and the
specific goods derived from it, and it is with respect
to this temporal common good and the goods derived
from it that the human virtue of fortitude is required.
As always in St. Thomas, grace is the perfection of
nature (*perfectio naturæ*).

There is a spiritual battle (*spiritualiter certando*) to
be fought for the conquest of eternal life: the kingdom of heaven requires fortitude, and it is the strong
who bear it away (*regnum cælorum vim patitur, et
violenti rapiunt illud*) [Matt. 11:12].[52] But there is also
a temporal battle to be waged for the realization of
the commandments of the Decalogue, "which are like
first principles, self-evident," — isn't the primacy of
the common good striking? — "and which have justice
as their object," that is, the duty to render to each
what is due him, in the first place union in view of
a common end: living in society, "a duty incumbent
on all." If the Decalogue does not mention the virtue
of fortitude, it is simply because the execution of its
commandments presupposes it more obviously than
its prescriptions explicitly state.[53]

The virtues related to fortitude, like fortitude itself,
have no other purpose than the defense and exemplifi-
cation of the natural and supernatural common good.

---

[52] Ibid., q. 140, art. 1, ad 1, where this verse is cited.
[53] Ibid., ad 3.

VI
CONCLUSION

I T MUST BE ACKNOWLEDGED THAT the magnitude of this task is immense, and that despite the totalitarian violence that tramples it underfoot and the liberal tolerance that vilifies it, the virtue of fortitude—which has vanished from the vocabulary of politicians and clergy alike— is today the quintessential virtue, without which a return to intellectual, aesthetic, moral, social, and religious health, now under attack on all sides, is absolutely impossible. Only now, at the end of this century, is it becoming clear—despite the delirious optimism, adrift and directionless, from *L'Avenir de la science* by Renan (1890)[1] to *Gaudium et Spes* of Vatican II (1965)—that we are entering the final phase of our civilization. Because we have substituted the *homo laborans* for *homo sapiens* and *homo politicus*, and in doing so turned our backs on the traditional teaching of the Catholic Church, the trajectory of this civilization is now irreversible.

Civilizations, of course, are mortal, yet at least those

---

[1] *The Future of Science*, on the importance of the history of religious origins. Ernest Renan (1823–1892), a religious skeptic, was a French Orientalist and historian of religion.

known to Europe, which have followed one another in the course of three millennia, had something human to transmit to those succeeding them, so that the reality of *the everlasting man* endured through their rises and falls, beyond their deaths.[2] If the industrial "civilization" which we have experienced endures through successive crises, from which it recovers only through inhuman wars, what will man living in it become, if not an *animal laborans*, living outside any true order, subjected from birth to death to the dominion of machines? And should this civilization disappear, what will be its legacy?

The answer is clear: *nothing*. Man ceases to be man in the ant colony of such a "civilization." He is not even bound to his fellow men by strong gregarious instincts that could automatically regulate his actions. He can certainly be integrated into a "hierarchy," though that is meaningless, since it happens automatically. And certainly, at least in theory, since one problem is resolved by replacing it with another and every step forward in one area means a step backward in another, technology continues to develop. Yet its complexity has reached the point where even the smallest error or accident, due to the interconnection of all the countless components in the system as a whole, can trigger a catastrophe. A single bolt is unloosened and the plane explodes!

It is not an exaggeration to claim that the more technology appears to unite men, the more it crams

[2] *The Everlasting Man* (1925) is the title of one of G. K. Chesterton's books.

them together within the solitude they experience as specialists, each unaware of the others. Adding to this is the fact that the ultimate purpose of all activity that transforms matter is subject to the immutable law of the economy, whether it is directed exclusively to individuals or to the collectivity — where this last term refers to individuals made in the same mold — and thus this activity can only create a latent dis-society: social conflicts are inherent to every "civilization" that is exclusively industrial.

But the individual is nothing, despite his imaginary claim (born out of his rupture with organic societies) to be everything. To bring together individuals thus isolated from each other, as we find in Augustin Cochin's conclusions,[3] more valid than ever, there is only *the socialization of thought* by means of myth, that is, through language stripped of all reference to reality, *the socialization of the person* caught in the gears of a machine-powered collective, and *the socialization of good* through the suction pump of a totalitarian state, which forces the person into deeper isolation. The three human activities, ordered in a hierarchy, *contemplation, action*, and *production* (now severed from its true purpose), no longer exist or no longer have any truly human meaning.

It is therefore necessary, from now on, before the

---

[3] French historian of the French Revolution (1876–1916; died in action in World War I). See his *La Révolution de la libre-pensée: la socialisation de la pensée (1759–1789), la socialisation de la personne (1789–1792), la socialisation des biens (1793–1794)* in *La Machine révolutionnaire* (2018), which contains nearly all of his works, most of which were published posthumously.

final collapse, and perhaps, if it pleases providence, to prevent it, to return to what is specifically and fundamentally proper to man: first, *to think*, and to think aright, to accept as true only what is true, that is, the data of sensory experience illuminated by the first principles of knowledge, themselves safeguarded by common sense; to renounce appearances that captivate us because they are products of the imagination, and because in them we discover our ego, deceptively aggrandized; to return to the natural metaphysics of the human mind. Then, *to act*, and to act rightly, to act in view of the common good of the community and the universal common good, which is the God of revelation, two distinct yet inseparable goods since the coming of Our Lord Jesus Christ. Finally, *to produce*, to make all the things necessary for the life of the individual, to improve them, to make them accessible to the greatest number, *but always under the governance of the common good, which orders them and subjects to itself the particular goods thus produced.* This primacy of the common good aims, above all, at the preservation of dynamic social relations, always threatened by the individualism inherent in economic activity.

This is something that cannot be achieved in a day, in ten years, or even in a century. *This is something that requires us to continually exercise the virtue of fortitude, from generation to generation*, as much to resist the evils engendered by all forms of decadence as to combat those who promote them, to allow the human plant to grow under the sun of God.

Both nature and God come to our aid. Nature has

always placed the remedy right alongside the evil. *Natura malorum remedia demonstrat.* A precise diagnosis is the first step towards healing. And God will never abandon the man who prays to Him. There are, in fact, privileged places inhabited by the few who resist the disease of the permanent revolution and who serve as starting points for renewal, since the supreme rule of technology, which destroys everything once left to itself, cannot destroy them without destroying itself. Technology will always need scientists and a minimum concern for the common good in order to produce its material goods and distribute them via a consumer market that is neither a free-for-all nor a military garrison. It is in the natural and semi-natural grassroots communities that the *realities* of daily life *resist*, despite everything, the revolutionary violence that seeks to annihilate them in order to replace them with constructs of the autonomous human mind, which would thereby consolidate its authority.

Undoubtedly, "the conditions for normal family and professional life are increasingly disappearing, tending ultimately to turn this life into hell."[4] Yet the day when the family and private enterprise no longer exist, and when organic social relations are entirely subordinated to relationships created by technology, will mark the end of the road for humanity. It will be the "end of history," the end of history, period. Unless, when these communities are completely infected by the permanent revolution which causes the hierarchy

[4] Louis Salleron in *Itinéraires*, January, 1972.

of human activities to be overthrown and withdrawn from them, the members of a family or an enterprise find themselves confronted with *realities* that must necessarily be imposed on them, *if they but look at them*, as a common good superior to the madness that could seduce them, a madness that tears down only to build something different.

It is all found in the attentive gaze on reality, on the actual things that form part of our daily existence, that cannot be separated from it without causing us suffering, and that, when we experience them, help us to flourish. Within the communities of our family and professional life, we occupy terrain where we can only be defeated if we hand it over to the enemy. This refers to the abandonment of the DUTIES OF OUR STATE IN LIFE, an expression that we hardly ever come across in modern discourse, particularly among the intelligentsia, penpushers who engage in idle chit-chat, and for good reason! This is our paramount obligation here below, which comes immediately after the duty to love God above all things, as enjoined on us by revelation, from which obligation *alone* derive all rights, provided that it is carried out. There is no right except the fulfillment of the duties of one's state in life and gathering the fruits that are born from it, which are never aborted except unintentionally. For we exist in the realm of action, and action attains its end only *ut in pluribus*, in most cases. [5]

[5] Original sin did not corrupt the social nature of man, but only wounded it. Our efforts, with the assistance of grace, are able to heal that wound.

The duties of one's state are what one is obliged to do in accordance with: the fixed, unchanging character of this state,[6] one's specific nature as man, and the fact that one belongs to a family and a country by birth, to a trade or profession by inclination or necessity. The duties of our state correspond *with our actual existence*, to which all our properly human activities refer. They allow no delegation of authority, no attenuation, no shirking on our part, lest we bring shame on ourselves. They are specific, continuing, unchanging, as is everything that pertains to nature.

No one can substitute for another within these small natural and semi-natural communities, from which we can separate ourselves only in thought, imagination, or action, but never *with respect to the person that we are*. I *belong* forever to this family, this profession, this homeland. In these societies, each person's place is determined by something that does not depend on him — by his entrance into existence on a particular day, in a particular place, by his vocation, by the response he gives to a call that transcends him and yet constitutes him, by inclinations whose inspiration arises from nature and which are directed by a rightly-formed will. Because our state cannot be separated from our existence, we must assume the task of fulfilling our duties of state, thereby realizing our being. *This requires, above all, actions inspired by the virtue of fortitude, which resists the seductions of*

---

[6] See the entries for *état* [state] in the Littré and Robert dictionaries. [De Corte is presumably referring to *Le Grand Robert*, much more extensive than *Le Petit Robert*.]

selfishness — which separates the Ego from the per-son — *and the enticements of the dis-society, as well as the opportunities for human weakness to come into play which strengthen modern liberal and socialist politics.*

Within these communities, the duties of one's state are always oriented towards the common good of its members. Far from opposing their respective well-being, they constitute it: working, for example, for the reputation and prosperity of the business of which one is a part brings with it personal recognition and mate-rial advantages. The temptation to selfishness, which none escape, is remedied by the conspicuous presence and monitoring of other members of the community. The obligations, sometimes demanding, imposed by the preservation of the common good do not involve stoic rigidity or heroism, but rather joy: is there any greater satisfaction than to have spent one's workday well, or to see one's children grow into true men and women? The exercise of the virtue of fortitude in carrying out the duties of one's state in life is always accompanied by a sense of satisfaction, despite the inevitable miseries of this life. Most people have for-gotten this under the burden of the dis-society, which thrusts them into the chaos of its ephemeral pleasures.

It is therefore necessary to struggle *with all one's might* against liberalism, whose starting point was the benevolent humanist concept that man, "the master of the world,"[7] bears within himself no seed of evil,

---

[7] So defined in *Gaudium et Spes* no. 12, blind before the crisis which was already fomenting in the course of Vatican II, as though there had been no original sin for the authors of this lengthy

and that everything corrupt in our existence is merely the result of unsound social systems that must be reformed. One must also combat socialism: "socialism of any type and shade leads to a total destruction of the human spirit and to a leveling of mankind into death."[8] The fortresses of natural micro-communities compel us to do this as an *absolute necessity*, if we wish to survive as rational animals and as political animals. Those who are willing must, through the spoken and written word, and above all by example, teach fathers, mothers, and family members the ABCs of the attitude to adopt: that the first word of resistance is NO. It cannot be repeated often enough: in the practical order, where action is directed towards its proper end, YES begins with NO. *The fundamental principles of family morality will follow.*

It is necessary to teach all producers, at all levels of business, *the rudiments of economic morality*. One does not produce for the sake of producing, nor in order to produce more and more. Wages, salaries, and profits are the recompense for services rendered to consumers. Consumers are human beings and they alone have the ability to find the balance between production and consumption, both in material and moral terms, provided that the market economy is regulated

tract, who surely had not worked on this compilation of all the modern forms of insanity by the sweat of their brow. [It should be noted that the document actually refers to man as the "master of all earthly creatures that he might subdue them and use them to God's glory."]

8 Solzhenitsyn, "A World Split Apart," Commencement address, Harvard University, June 8, 1978.

by moral standards and a legal code that a true state, guardian of the public good, enforces against the assaults of parasites obsessed with their own assets.[9] "Socialism with a human face" is an illusion, a hoax. Money is a means and not an end. Property is private in nature and communal in its use and in its products. The collective ownership of the means of production is camouflage for a "new ruling class," next to which the most oppressive form of capitalism appears as a liberator. Communism, no matter what muddleheaded bishops may say, who cast a concupiscent glance at it, is "intrinsically perverse," etc.

These fundamentals, as clear as day, confirmed a thousand times over by experience, call for the virtue of fortitude in its twofold form: *sustinere* and *aggredi*, to endure and to attack.

In the humble acts of daily life where there are still some glimmers of the true nature of man and of his virtuous actions ordered to the common good, we also find the very breath of truth: the natural and Christian law as taught by the Gospel and by the pre-conciliar Church. Without fixing one's gaze on this star, our course on earth becomes impossible in the dark night we are now going through. This is the situation, and in those privileged environments, where we can still act effectively and transmit the fruits of our activity, by holding *firm* to both the

[9] Our late friend Henri de Lovinfosse [1897–1977, a Belgian entrepreneur] put this into practice in his actions and writings. His factories, in the course of more than half a century, have not stopped functioning for a single hour due to strikes.

natural and supernatural we will be able to make our way through the intermediate stages and with patience restore society and the Church. To the unrestricted emancipation of man through an omnipotent technology, which, deprived of the sovereign lights of the True and the Good, has only one escape hatch, subversive violence and the permanent revolution, to the consequent destruction of man's fundamental nature, there is only one response: perseverance in the restoration of the rational and social animal within ourselves, *by means of the virtue of fortitude and the outward acts* that direct it towards its end.

The simple yet moving story told by Ramuz in *Derborence*[10] illustrates the realism of the virtue of fortitude in the most humble of men, who are yet the closest to earth and heaven at one and the same time. Some shepherds have gone up to their mountain chalets above the clouds, to tend their flocks during the summer. One night, the mountain behind the sheepfold collapses. Just one shepherd escapes from the avalanche. He finds himself buried beneath a huge mass of rock. For two months, he survives on dry bread and water seeping out from the debris. He probes into the rock and hollows a way out, cutting up his hands, at times feeling defeated, yet always victorious over his own seeming defeat. He finally emerges into

---

[10] Novel by the Swiss writer Charles Ferdinand Ramuz, 1936. We previously cited this parable at the end of our *Essai sur la fin d'une civilisation* (*On the Death of a Civilization*, Arouca Press, 2023), but without looking at it in light of natural and supernatural fortitude.

the daylight, mute, stammering, spectral. For he wants
to live. His home needs him. His home awaits him.
He goes down to the village, where the people are
startled before this phantom. The priest goes to meet
him, armed with a cross. His wife approaches, then
stops. "And after looking at him closely, though at
a distance, as though she dared not draw near, said:

"'Oh, Antoine, is it you?'

"'Just touch me, this is my skin, my flesh, *now that
I have borne the cross* . . . Just touch me,' he said, 'you'll
see, *I'm not an invention of your mind, I'm solid, I
won't go away, it's me.*'

"'Oh!' she said, 'Is it possible?'"

The future belongs to the magnanimity of the
humble, to their inexhaustible fortitude.